THE MAR
MILITARY IN THE BIBLE

Joyce Schroeder
with RADM Curt Kemp, USN

a book by

MALACHI PRESS

Copyright © 2024 Joyce Schroeder
All rights reserved.
JoyceSchroeder.com

All Scripture quotations, unless otherwise indicated, are taken from the Holy Bible, New International Version®, NIV®. Copyright ©1973, 1978, 1984, 2011 by Biblica, Inc.™ Used by permission of Zondervan. All rights reserved worldwide. www.zondervan.com The "NIV" and "New International Version" are trademarks registered in the United States Patent and Trademark Office by Biblica, Inc.™

Design by Kimberly Lamb Creative, LLC

ISBN 978-0-9963303-6-7

The military is a challenging work environment that absorbs and responds to the world's bad news. This book ministers to anyone connected to that lifestyle of service (serving, retired, and family) who could use some good news to strengthen dignity and resolve. The comfort Jesus Christ offers fills up the uncertainties of military working conditions, including the ache of being away from loved ones and the search for a deeper identity that will outlast military service. Joyce makes clear in this book how God views, values, and uses those who serve to display his character of peace, justice, and love to each other and to our broken world.
—Captain (Retired) Jazmine Lawrence, Air Combat Systems Officer, Royal Canadian Air Force

The military has so much more to offer our world than simply the mission given to them by the government. In fact, throughout the Bible, God uses the role and lifestyle of a soldier to illustrate His truths about being a follower of Jesus. In this book, Joyce brings to life these themes and weaves them together in ways that will help all Christians, military or not, understand more fully what it looks like to be "in step" with Jesus.
—Brian Kleager, VP for Strategic Partnerships and PR, Cadence International, Former Armor Officer and Combat Veteran, United States Army

A must-read for anyone serving in the Armed Forces, trying to navigate that world according to God's Word. The Bible provides much guidance in this area, and thanks to Joyce's efforts, it is now accessible in one clear, succinct, and masterfully written volume.
—Stan Fisher, PhD, U.S. Naval Officer and Author of *Sustaining the Carrier War: The Deployment of U.S. Naval Air Power to the Pacific*

Joyce offers us a book that is birthed out of her deep love for the military and the gospel. Each word is intentional and allows us to see God's Kingdom through new eyes—ones that acknowledge the battle times we are living and understand the platform that his story was designed on. In our current culture, military battles often conjure up graphic and painful images. Through her wisdom, Joyce paints the picture of how God used the military, military leaders, and battles as he established his people and his power. And we are left with deep hope that he has not abandoned us today.
—Stacy Follis-Wiens, Director of Communications, Cadence International

Having worked with Joyce Schroeder for over 30 years in military ministry, she is eminently qualified to explore the Bible and its use of military. You will find this work astonishing in its comprehensive approach to how the military is discussed throughout the various books of the Bible.
—Dr. Jim Howard, Sr. Pastor, Dillon Community Church, and adjunct faculty, Denver Seminary Doctor of Ministry program

The March and Music of Military in the Bible *invites the reader to fall more in love with God's Word and the military. Those two are not always the most obvious of pairings, but Joyce Schroeder's deep affection is infectious. The result is a growing appreciation for, comprehension of, and identification with the military in the Story of God.*
—Mike Paterson, MA, LMHC, Cadence International Pastoral Care

Dedication

To my parents, Dick and Margaret Patty,
now in heaven.
Who faithfully walked with God.
Who were some of the Founders of Cadence International
and spent their adult lives in ministry to the military.
Who believed, lived, and shared the gospel.
Who loved people generously.
Who were Kingdom allies to me and my brothers,
and to our families and friends.

And to the six who were also
Founders of OCSC/Cadence International,
Faithful in their march and music
of life and ministry.
Jesse and Nettie Miller
Tom and Dotty Hash
C.P. and Alma Tarkington

I gladly follow in your steps.
Cadence.org/History

And to David, with whom I am honored to share a foxhole.

Table of Contents

Introduction i

SECTION 1: Biblical **Characteristics** of the Military **1**
Chapter 1: Presence 3
Chapter 2: Purpose 9
Chapter 3: People Group 19
Chapter 4: Professional 27
Chapter 5: Positioned 35
Chapter 6: Portrayal 45

SECTION 2: Callings **53**
Chapter 7: Christian Soldiers 55
Chapter 8: Stand Your Ground 61
Chapter 9: Reveille, Retreat, and Taps 71

SECTION 3: Courage **79**
Chapter 10: Conquering King 81
Chapter 11: Jesus Loves Me 87
Chapter 12: Until Then 95

Acknowledgments 105
Appendix A: Thoughts on the Bible 107
Appendix B: The Kingdom of Heaven 111
Bibliography 117
About the Authors 121

Introduction

"GOODNIGHT TOM, GOODNIGHT George, goodnight Chief . . ." I said as I waved my little three-year-old hand like a princess to the sailors I knew by name, their white uniforms filling the large gathering room of the Subic Service Center near Subic Bay in Olongapo, Philippines. While our dad mingled with servicemen, my younger brother and I walked up the stairs with our mom to have nightly devotions, and we prayed for those sailors by name.

My parents, Dick and Margaret Patty, were some of the missionary founders of OCSC/Cadence International.[1] I was born on their first furlough back to the U.S. and traveled by car through many states in my early months as my folks reported to ministry partners across the country. I celebrated my first birthday on a ship heading back to the Philippines and got my "sea legs" as I learned to walk on that ship. Then I had to learn to walk again once we were on dry land.

It was during one of our nightly devotions at Subic that I, not yet four years old, knelt by the bed and said, "Dear Jesus, please come into my heart." With sincere faith and simple trust, I meant that prayer—and Jesus meant his answer, "Yes!" He has been in me and with me ever since and will be mine forever. For as long as I can remember, I have longed for everyone else in the world to know and love him too.

I am a civilian; I have never served in the military. But two themes—military people and the gospel—beat in my heart.

Growing up I witnessed story after story of how God took men and women's time in the military and used it to set the trajectory of their lives to make a difference for him in all kinds of ways all over the world.

---

1 OCSC was the abbreviation of Overseas Christian Servicemen's Centers.

It wasn't until a few years ago that I became more intrigued with the military activity in the Bible. In many ways, I knew they were in the background of God's story, but I have come to see that military people also feature more significantly throughout. My hope is that in reading this book you will also develop a greater understanding and appreciation of the military's significance and how it might affect you and your story.

Please understand that I am not writing here about being militant or militaristic. This is not about Christian nationalism, activism, or pacifism. I hope the difference will become clear. Further, I must state emphatically at the outset: war is tragic. It is not something any of us want our loved ones or our country to go through. And yet, it is with us on this earth, along with its resulting global suffering.

Maybe you are in the military and you have had this quiet but ongoing question in the back of your mind: "Can I really please God and also serve in the armed forces?" I believe you can. Perhaps you have never been in the military and you wonder what relevance a discussion of the military and the Bible has to do with you. The answer is the impetus of this study: I believe every Christian is called to be a mature spiritual-military person.

TIMES AND TERMS

The Bible does not have the same categories or branches for the military as many countries do today. In Bible times in the Ancient Near East, military branch distinctions were swordsmen, horsemen, spearmen, archers, and slingers.[2] The military was generally referred to as an army, and military personnel were called soldiers. Military officers were distinguished as soldiers or centurions.

If you are in the armed forces, you know your identity—you know your country, your branch, your MOS or MOSID, your rank, and your mission.[3] Please accept "soldier," "army," "commander," and "military community" for the general terms they represent and look for where you would best fit in as we go along.

---

2   Stephen Leston, *Illustrated Guide to Bible Battles*, 6.
3   MOS stands for Military Occupational Specialty in the U.S. and MOSID stands for Military Occupation Structure Identification Code in Canada.

This book was birthed from personal Bible study. It is not an academic treatise. As a doctoral student in my thesis phase at Denver Seminary, I understand the difference. Both are valuable, and I offer these words as my research thus far.

MARCH AND MUSIC

My husband David and I serve with Cadence International. It is a ministry formed in 1954 with a sole focus on the military and their dependents. Our mission is "sharing the gospel and our lives with the military community," referring to Paul's beautiful ministry description in 1 Thessalonians 2:8. We had the privilege of being part of pioneering Malachi Ministries in the 1980s, now called Cadence Student Ministries. David has served as the president of Cadence since 1995.

Over the years I've heard David describe the name "Cadence" as both a marching and a musical term—keeping in step with the Spirit of God (Galatians 5:25) and proclaiming the salvation and glory of the Lord day in and day out in a way that reaches all people (Psalm 96:1–3). Marching keeps us together, like the cadence of troops in sync as they travel as one unit. Though some military branches don't march, this movement also implies intentional unity. Music makes our message winsome—which it truly is—and helps us remember that which is true (the way lyrics and melodies loop in your head).

> Because we loved you so much, we were delighted to share with you not only the gospel of God but our lives as well.
> **1 THESSALONIANS 2:8**

This book is a cadence of sorts, a reflection on the march—the cohesive themes, messaging, and imagery—of military in the Bible and how that might affect Christians today. It is also a reflection of the musical soundtracks of God's Story and a way of remembering—like lyrics and tunes—how the military stories in the Bible connect with our current callings.

You will see that I often capitalize the word "Story." I do this when referring to the grand narrative of the Bible—God's Story—one that factors into each of our life stories, and in which our stories have a part. It also helps me as I offer this study and pray that it matters to you. Just as Jesus took me seriously when I asked to belong to him, he also takes our offerings and our stories seriously. As it turns out, they all matter in the continuing Story and the grand scheme of things.

WHAT TO EXPECT

There are three sections to this book. The first looks at biblical **characteristics** of the military. Here we will get a glimpse into some of the military people and stories of the Bible. I'll present six general characteristics that I see in military people of the Bible that are still true of military members today. This section will give us a lay of the land regarding the relevance of this topic to the movement and mission of God.

The second section will take us into the civilian realm—but it is also important for those in uniform. Here we will look at God's **callings** for each of us to be spiritual soldiers and engage in spiritual warfare. Spiritual pacifism is not an option for those who follow Jesus, and we would be wise to be prepared.

The third section is one I hope will bring us **courage** as well as encouragement. Because no matter how the first two sections become narrated in our lives, we know how this Story ends. We know Who is the victorious King. We know how and why we can make it through our battles and our journeys . . . and still be at peace.

This book is not an exhaustive treatment of military activity in the Bible or biblical characteristics of the military. It is designed to be a prompting and an inspiration that will help take us a little further down the road of understanding the depth of God's heart, his Word, his ways, and his call on our lives.

JOINING US

I am honored to introduce to you Rear Admiral Curt Kemp, a retired officer of the United States Navy. A graduate of the U.S. Naval Academy, Admiral Kemp served for 34 years as a Surface Warfare Officer. My husband David first met Curt in Japan while visiting The Lighthouse, a Cadence ministry. We got to know him better when he served as a member and then Chair of the Cadence International Board of Directors. More biographical details are located at the end of this book.

RADM Kemp will be joining us for the journey through this Bible study, especially in the first section, though he was one of the editors for the entire manuscript. His sections are titled **The Admiral's Corner** and offer first-hand insights from his years of military service and walking with God.

Many others joined me in the creation of this book, each one contributing wisdom and care for its message. Please see the Acknowledgments page for brief introductions.

Now, let's dive in!

SECTION 1

Biblical **Characteristics** of the Military

The military is woven through the Bible from beginning to end. Why does its march and music matter in the narrative of the past and to our lives today? Whether military or civilians, the biblical characteristics of the military call for our understanding and response, which we will explore throughout this book.

CHAPTER 1

Presence

BEGIN TO LOOK at the military in the Bible and you will see that they are there—they are **present**. They are a constant, showing up from the beginning to the end of this book. Throughout history, around the world, in every country, and through the Bible, the military has been there, is here, and will be present in the future—until the end of earth-time. Why is this so? The reality of the continual presence of military forces is a persistent indicator that all is not well on our planet, and we are part of the problem and the solution.

BEGINNING OF BATTLE

God's Story (again, I capitalize Story here as it arches over all stories) given to us in the Bible starts with light, with beauty, and with loving relationship. The human story begins with the Triune God—Father, Son, and Holy Spirit—his image, desire, and creative activity. It continues with his earth-dust, his very breath, and his blessing. If you haven't read Genesis 1 and 2 in a while, I suggest you pause and read it now.

As you read, consider what it looks like, smells like, feels like, and sounds like in these chapters. If you were to write a movie score for the music that accompanies these chapters, what chord progressions and percussive elements describe this dynamic beginning?

In the first two chapters of Genesis, God creates the world and everything in it, including a man and a woman made to be his image. Old Testament professor Dr. Carmen Joy Imes writes, "God is not usually visible, so he appoints humans to remind creation and each other of his presence."[1] God plants a beautiful, tasty, and well-watered garden in Eden. He places the humans in that garden with his instructions for their well-being and flourishing. Yet the garden is not a completely safe place. There is danger and an enemy in Eden, and there will be choices in Eden. "You are free to eat from any tree in the garden; but you must not eat from the tree of the knowledge of good and evil, for when you eat of it you will surely die" (Genesis 2:16–17).

"You are free . . ." This is how much *respect* God gives the humans he made in his image. In the beginning, and now, he does not violate the trust he placed in them to make their own decisions. "But you must not . . ." This is how much *care* God gives the humans he made as his image. In the beginning, and now, he clearly sets forth the path of life—flourishing life on the planet and eternal life in heaven—and he implores them to choose this path.

Then Genesis 3 follows. Tragically, in the beginning and to this day, we humans made in God's image use our freedom to choose paths of destruction that deceptively appeal and fuel our arrogance.[2] The humans in the garden chose to listen to the lure of the enemy rather than trust the voice of their Creator. We call that choice against God "sin."

What happens next could seem judgmental on God's part. In fact, it is. But look at what else is included in the curses and the exile from Eden. The first thing the humans recognize after they defiantly (Adam) and deceivingly (Eve) disobey God's instruction to not eat from the tree of the knowledge of good and evil is that they are naked. This is not news to the reader because we were told in Genesis 2:25 that they were naked—and they felt no shame.

The subsequent rush to sew fig leaves together to try to cover themselves up indicates that an immediate consequence of not choosing God's

---

1 Carmen Joy Imes, *Being God's Image: Why Creation Still Matters*, 31. Quoted with permission from the author.
2 See Genesis 3:6.

way was shame.[3] Christian Psychiatrist Curt Thompson writes, "From the beginning it has been God's purpose for this world to be one of emerging goodness, beauty, and joy. Evil has wielded shame as a primary weapon to see to it that that world never happens."[4]

Notice what God does first in response to the humans' disobedience. He walks in the garden. He comes to them, moves toward them, and does *not* initially ask, "What have you done?"—but *rather*, "Where are you?" As our friend and Bible scholar Jim Howard puts it, "God's first move is about relationship, not punishment. He pursues them when they are no longer able to pursue him."[5]

Next, we learn that the humans not only feel shame, but they also feel fear. Something is terribly broken, and though they now have experiential knowledge of good and evil, they don't know how to fix their sin, shame, and fear. But God does not expect them to fix it. He knows they are not that powerful. God is the only one with all power and he uses it to start his Story of Redemption—his dealing with sin, shame, brokenness, and pain.

I was watching some of our grandchildren one evening while their parents went out on a date. After I'd tucked them into bed, four-year-old Landon got out of bed and came across the hall to chat with me. During our short conversation, out of the blue he said, "Sometimes I do bad things and my parents take a toy away for a while. It's called a consequence. I get consequences for doing bad things." I replied that this meant that his parents loved him and were not going to let him get away with doing bad things. Then a couple of minutes later I asked him, "Do you think it will be okay with your parents if they come home now and find you out of bed?" It wasn't long before he said, "I'm going back to bed now. Goodnight, Grandma." And he didn't get out of bed again.

As much as we do not like it when there are consequences, or judgment, for our wrongdoing, we sure don't want anyone else on the planet to get away with doing wrong and not being punished. Imagine the fear we would live under if there were never consequences for crimes or if no brokenness could ever be repaired, redeemed, or restored. Talk about utter despair!

---

3 This is a clue that the fruit they ate was likely a fig.
4 Curt Thompson, *The Soul of Shame*, 13.
5 Conversation with Dr. Jim Howard, May 2021.

God starts his judgment with the enemy himself: Satan, also known as the devil, in the form of a serpent. God puts him in his place, face down on his belly on the ground eating dust (the dust indicating the sentence of death). We will talk more about this enemy later, but for now we see that he has nothing on the majesty and power of God Almighty. Furthermore, some theologians see the first prophecy of the Savior, Jesus, stated here in Genesis 3:15. The enemy will be given enough power to strike the heel of humanity and their Messiah. But the Messiah, who is born from a woman in the genealogical line of these humans who disobeyed, will crush the serpent Satan's head. Others note that while this might not be a direct prophecy about Jesus, it describes the "continual, unresolved conflict between humans and the representatives of evil."[6] Eating dust, crushed head—this judgment is from the hands of God who is love.

Also ultimately loving are the punishments on the man and woman. Life is not going to be easy for them. God's creation intention and commission given to them together—be the image of God, be fruitful and multiply, and rule and subdue the earth—does *not* change but will always include hardship and struggle. Perhaps now they won't be as eager to let appearances deceive and arrogance demand.

Let us note here that the curse given by God is directly on the devil and on the ground, which then falls indirectly on the people. They will have to deal with a cursed enemy and a cursed home all their lives. Another way to say it is that humans will live under the curse. The late theologian Dr. Ray Anderson put it this way, "Contrary to conventional thinking, the humans were never cursed, only their relation to the earth."[7]

To understand the concepts of blessing and cursing more fully, a few quotes are helpful. From the NIV Application Commentary, Dr. John Walton writes, "To bless someone is to put that person under God's protection, enjoying God's favor. To curse is to remove from God's protection and favor."[8] Furthermore, the curse of Genesis 3 is ultimately an act of grace. As our nephew and Cambridge doctoral student Tyler Patty puts it, "When transgression disrupts the order of creation and rebellion ruptures

---

6 John Walton, *The NIV Application Commentary: Genesis*, 226.
7 Ray Anderson, *Minding God's Business*, 137.
8 Walton, 229.

the relationship between God and his creatures, God speaks to right that which has been wronged. . . . God's purposes never end with curse, but always look beyond it."[9]

God himself then makes Adam and Eve more suitable clothing for their nakedness out of a skin. In this he offers remedy for their newly experienced shame. God is the one to shed blood, the symbol of life, for the covering of his people—an animal's blood, and then later, his own.

Finally, God takes extreme action to prevent the humans from eating of the tree of life, from which they were free to eat beforehand. Now that they know both good and evil, to eat from the tree of life would evidently keep them in the condition of knowing evil forever. Since God's eternal intention for his people does not include evil, he banishes them from Eden and sets cherubim and a flaming sword—supernatural creatures, perhaps military angels, and a weapon—at the entrance to guard the humans' original home.[10]

God himself is the first one to use military force in the Bible.

God himself is the last one to use military force in the Bible.[11]

EDEN TO HEAVEN

Throughout the Bible we encounter military forces sent by God and military forces who represent enemies of God. We read stories of good guys and bad guys. We wrestle with military destruction of people and places which are, or appear to be, innocent victims. We wonder why it seems there is never peace on earth, and we battle with evil inside our very own hearts. Is there not always some kind of conflict going on?

What we often hear termed as "The Fall" in Genesis 3 is part of the beginning of God's Story, of humans' stories, and the story of Redemption. The Fall includes the presence of an enemy, the disobedience of humans, the effects of the curse, and the resulting brokenness and power struggles in relationships. Because of The Fall, we not only have militaries, but we also have doctors, lawyers, pastors, politicians, counselors, security forces, sanitation workers, and many other professions.

---

9 Tyler Patty, "Curse and the Power of Blessing: A Linguistic Study of Genesis 1-11," 67, 163.
10 See Genesis 3:22-24.
11 See Revelation 20.

We live on a beautiful and broken planet. It will never be perfect. There is still a flaming sword keeping us out of Eden. But we need not despair.

God, the righteous Judge, has made provision for our covering and healing of our shame. He himself came to earth, forever connected to humanity by becoming a human. Jesus took care of the curse and the enemy once and for all by his death on a cross. The path that leads to death was swallowed up in the resurrection of Jesus. He conquered death itself.

> Just as people are destined to die once, and after that to face judgment, so Christ was sacrificed once to take away the sins of many; and he will appear a second time, not to bear sin, but to bring salvation to those who are waiting for him.
> **HEBREWS 9:27–28**

A new heaven and the new earth—where no sin, shame, pain, suffering, or death is allowed—is awaiting all who let God cover them with the blood of Jesus. Military angels guard that entrance as well.[12] A battle unlike any other is yet to come when our enemy Satan is dealt his final crushing. Until then, we can live in hope and in victory—yes, military victory. We'll talk about that more.

RECAP

The military is present—then and now—because there is constant battle in the world between good and evil. All of humanity was impacted by The Fall, and we experience resulting tension and ruptures with God and between each other. The military, like other professions, has an ongoing part in the protection and flourishing of people on the planet while we are between Eden and heaven.

---

12 See Revelation 15:5–8; 17; 19:12–14, 22:1–11.

CHAPTER 2

Purpose

SOLDIERS ARE NOT randomly scattered throughout the pages of the Bible or the movements of history. Their presence is purposeful. It does not condone lifestyles of violence nor do they truncate the encompassing power that God possesses and deploys in any way he chooses at any time. Further, military presence and purpose share recurring examples of the ways God allows all kinds of vocations to function with meaning in this world.

NUMBERS MATTER

When studying a book of the Bible, a chapter, or a set of verses, we consider repeated words and themes, along with textual and cultural context, sentence structure, cross references, and other Bible study resources. Bible content is not random, nor is it poorly written. There is meaning and method in every part.[1]

This is why, when we look at the sheer volume of military people, terms, battles, and presence, we can assume God means for us to understand

---

[1] Perhaps you've heard that when something in the Bible is repeated three times—a word, a command, a warning—it is for emphasis. Three times means this is important, imperative, intentional. For example, the phrase "Holy, holy, holy is the Lord God Almighty" in Isaiah 6:3 and Revelation 4:8 is constructed in this way because the triple repetition of "holy" takes us to the highest imaginable level of righteousness, purity, integrity, and awe. Yes, God is more holy than a triple praise can describe. But saying it three times communicates even more than just the repeated word.

something important here. Let's pay attention to the repeated weaving of military into God's Story.

Thanks to accessible Bible study resources like BibleGateway, Logos, Accordance Bible software, and others, one can quite quickly search various Bible translations for words and their meanings. The numbers and references I will use, unless noted, are from the New International Version (NIV 2011) translation since it is widely trusted and the one with which I am most familiar. It is helpful to note that in cross referencing other translations, such as ESV and NASB, the numbers are similar to the NIV. As I share these numbers, I understand I am not covering every base there is to cover in Bible word studies regarding the military. However, the glimpse we get here gives us an emphasis we cannot ignore.

Soldiers appear at least 90 times and in 26 books of the Bible. The word commander shows up 182 times in 22 books of the Bible. Centurions (officers in charge of 80–100 soldiers) are noted 23 times in the New Testament. The word army is used 258 times in 22 books of the Bible. And the New Living Translation (NLT) translates Lord Almighty and Lord of Hosts as "LORD of Heaven's Armies" 268 times.

Other words and numbers we may consider are: sword–406, arrow–60, siege–53, shield–95, armor–41, ambush–28, weapon–44, chariot–154, enemy–112, warrior or war–287, and victory–41. In his book, *Illustrated Guide to Bible Battles*, Stephen Leston explores the details of over 90 Scriptural battles, covering military heroes and villains, battle synopses, and weapons information.[2]

In more than one third of the 66 books of the Bible, the military is part of the narrative. They show up throughout Scripture!

PURPOSES AND FUNCTIONS

One of the more difficult purposes for most of us to reconcile is that God sometimes uses the military to **carry out his judgment** on a group of people. Numbers 31 can be a troublesome passage, but it is not the only passage like it. Verses 1–3 say, "The Lord said to Moses, 'Take vengeance on the

---

2 Leston, *Illustrated Guide to Bible Battles*.

Midianites for the Israelites. After that, you will be gathered to your people.' So Moses said to the people, 'Arm some of your men to go to war against the Midianites so that they may carry out the Lord's vengeance on them.'"

Seminary professors Dr. William Webb and Dr. Gordon Oeste took fourteen years to write their book, *Bloody, Brutal, and Barbaric?*[3] In it they present six theses that each shed light on the historical and cultural aspects of war in the Bible as well as the incremental redemptive movement of God against the backdrop of Ancient Near Eastern societies. They suggest that God's love and justice are not separate but intersecting.[4] And that "in the realm of human ethics, numerous examples of the most loving action include at least some degree of potential for or engagement in violent force."[5] This book is a technical, brilliant, and thorough work. I respectfully quote from it acknowledging that the context of the whole is needed to fully understand a quote. I highly recommend reading its 400 pages if you wish to dig deep into this complex subject.

In the Bible book of Joshua, a narrative full of military activity, God instructs the army of Israel to conquer land that he set apart for his people. History has demonstrated how this concept can be wrongly used, as in the case of the Crusades. But that does not diminish the fact that a purpose for which God has used militaries is to **shape the boundaries of people and countries** (See also Acts 17:26–27).

Some 850 years after Joshua, Ezra was processing the fact that he had not asked the king for soldiers and horsemen to protect them as they traveled because he wanted to show that God would protect them (Ezra 8:21–23). This passage affirms, rather than negates, the fact that militaries are **often needed to protect people.**

Fast forward another 550 years to Acts 21:27–40, and it was Roman soldiers who kept Paul from being beaten to death and who then gave him a platform to speak to the crowd. While we know that any kind of armed force can be, and sometimes is, used irresponsibly and for evil, a righteous purpose of the military is to **maintain order and promote peace.**[6]

---

3 Webb and Oeste, *Bloody, Brutal, and Barbaric?* 11, 13. Quoted with permission from the authors.
4 Webb and Oeste, 308.
5 Webb and Oeste, 318.
6 I commend to you chapter 2 of Esau McCaulley's *Reading While Black*.

In an airport, I recently saw a large advertisement encouraging those who walked by to emulate a famous woman because she is a "force for good." This ad was about one powerful person and how she uses that power. Military people are not focused on being powerful individuals, but they are powerful as a collective force. In addition to maintaining order and promoting peace, another military purpose is to function as a **force for good**. This can include visible assurance to friends and allies, deterrence to those who might do harm, and humanitarian assistance. I see this purpose of "force for good" reflected and referenced throughout Scripture and affirmed through many conversations with military people.

MILITARY FIGURES OF THE OLD TESTAMENT: ABRAM, MOSES, AND JOSHUA

Let us now become more familiar with some of the specific stories of military in the Bible and how they relate to these purposes.

Abram

The first war in the Bible is the War of the Kings in Genesis 14. While we may not think of Abram as a military man, he highlights the purpose of protecting people as he leads 318 trained soldiers on a night raid to rescue his relative Lot, his family, and Lot's belongings. Abram and his troops are successful in defeating four allied kings and accomplishing their mission.

It is noted in this battle, as well as throughout the conflicts God leads or allows his people to go into, that God's activity is the deciding factor in the victory. As the priest Melchizedek prays in his blessing over Abram in Genesis 14:20: "And blessed be God Most High, who delivered your enemies into your hand."

Moses

In Exodus, we learn that Moses was a man born to Hebrews and raised in the court of Egypt's Pharaoh, which along with other royals, likely included military training. But we do not directly see his military involvement until much later in life. For 40 of his adult years, he worked as a shepherd in

Midian, where he escaped Egypt after killing an Egyptian who was harming a Hebrew, for which Moses was almost put to death.[7]

Then when Moses was 80 (an uncommon age for military recruitment!) he was called up to confront Pharaoh and join God in rescuing the Hebrew people (also called Israelites) from oppression. God instructed Moses to boldly demand the release of the Hebrews. The ten forthcoming plagues—also attacks on the Egyptians' pagan gods—verified the demand was from God Almighty.[8]

Then Moses, with a leadership team including his brother Aaron and his sister Miriam, led the Hebrews out of Egypt (and then through another 40 years in the wilderness).[9] They could see Egyptians still on their heels after they crossed the Red Sea on the dry land God provided. The Israelites were terrified. Moses' battle cry at that moment can still encourage us today: "Do not be afraid. Stand firm and you will see the deliverance the LORD will bring you today. The Egyptians you see today you will never see again. The LORD will fight for you; you need only to be still" (Exodus 14:13-14).[10] In addition to his first history-changing battle, Numbers 20, 21, and 31 give other examples of military battles fought by the Israelites with Moses in command.

Moses was the human author of the Pentateuch or Torah, the first five books of the Bible, given by God during the "wilderness years" after the rescue from Egypt.[11] Psalm 90 is also attributed to Moses. As a Westerner, I have sometimes looked on those 40 years after the exodus as sad, maybe even wasted, wandering years for Moses and the Israelites. But I realized I needed to change my perspective. Because God was establishing his people in that time—a reset and recalibration—as he revealed himself to them, tangibly led them, and strengthened and prepared them for the tasks ahead that would require great faith and obedience. God set up his tent—the tabernacle as visible presence—making his home among them. Books of the Bible came to us from those 40 wilderness years. Wasted? No way. God is always at work.

---

7 See Exodus 2:11-15.
8 Tremper Longman, *How to Read Exodus*, 107-111.
9 See Micah 6:4.
10 Read the story for yourself in Exodus 13 and 14.
11 Note: Some scholars place the writing of Genesis during the exile in the 700s B.C. rather than after the Exodus around 1400 B.C. The four following books of the Torah are generally attributed to Moses.

THE ADMIRAL'S CORNER

Spot Promotion
Foster child, prince, escapee, shepherd, statesman, leader, administrator, judge, military commander. Moses had an unusual and long path before assuming his military duties. Near the end of his life, he established an army divided into military units based on tribes. Using the various tribes, a 360-degree "defense-in-depth" formation was established around the holy Tabernacle, both for when the Israelites were camped or on the move. Although perhaps lacking significant military training, Moses was "spot-promoted" by the Lord to the position of General over this army. As part of his responsibilities, Moses communicated to his troops the "laws of warfare" passed down from God.

One of the last great works Moses accomplished before he died, recorded in Numbers 1, was organizing an army to move forward into the promised land. Along with that, he communicated God's specific instructions for warfare in Deuteronomy 20. In Moses' varied military activity, he highlights the military purposes of shaping the boundaries of people, protecting people and their allegiance to God, at times carrying out God's judgment, as well as maintaining order and promoting peace.

Joshua
Joshua was a military man through and through. His adolescence and young adulthood were spent as Moses' assistant, then second-in-command. He served as a key military General, and an entire book of the Bible with his name is devoted to battles, conquests, and division of land. The battle of Jericho in Joshua 6 is perhaps the most distinct example of the *march* and *music* of military in the Bible. It is also important to note that we learn from a phrase in Exodus 33:11b that Joshua was intentional about his own spiritual formation as a young man. "Joshua, son of Nun, did not leave the tent." I wrote about this passage in a blog, reflecting that, "Joshua not only wanted to witness and participate in the mighty

acts of God, I think he also wanted to hear God for Himself."[12]

Joshua 1:1–9 is a passage I've memorized with friends.[13] However, when we learned it, we left out verse 4. It didn't seem to have the rhythm and roll of the other verses. But that is not to say that Joshua 1:4 is unimportant. In fact, it is in some ways an overview of battles that follow in this book. As noted earlier, the book of Joshua highlights the purpose of militaries to shape the boundaries of people groups and land.

> Your territory will extend from the desert to Lebanon, and from the great river, the Euphrates—all the Hittite country—to the Mediterranean Sea in the west.
> **JOSHUA 1:4**

The detailed military activity in Joshua leads us into difficult subjects like the biblical concept of "herem"—a transliterated Hebrew word meaning property consecrated solely to God— and the question of "holy wars."[14] There are no easy answers for these complex subjects, but there is much to learn about God's heart for his people and for the world in these difficult passages.[15]

What we know for sure about Joshua is that he was a man of God. Though human and thus not perfect, Joshua was one of a handful of people in the Bible of whom a negative character trait is not described.[16] Some might see compromised character in the situation in Joshua 9 where he was deceived by the Gibeonites and made a peace treaty with them though his people did not first consult the Lord regarding these visitors. However, I see that as a negative action rather than a negative character description. Joshua did not violate that treaty after he found out the Gibeonites' true identity. He assigned them to difficult labor, but it was labor that was part of provision for the worship of God—wood cutters and water carriers for the assembly and the altar. In that sense he was giving them the opportunity to get close to where God met his people, a

---

[12] Joyce Schroeder, "Joshua and the Tent," JoyceSchroeder.com.
[13] See other passages you can memorize with me at JoyceSchroeder.com/Bible-memory.
[14] See Joshua chapters 6, 8, 10, and 11.
[15] See "Joshua and the Ethics of War" in the NIV First-Century Study Bible.
[16] Others we could consider in this realm are Caleb, Daniel, Joseph, Mary, Lydia, Priscilla, and more.

THE ADMIRAL'S CORNER

Joshua: The Ideal XO

Joshua, a classic military man, worked his way up through the ranks over a 40-year period as the second-in-command and represents the best traits of a "servant leader." Due to his extensive and challenging experience in battles, he may have been a better military commander than Moses. But he exemplified humility, never lost sight of his positional responsibilities, and remained loyal to both Moses and the Lord in carrying out his challenging duties. His strong faith enabled him to patiently wait until God showed him that his time had come to become the General, which is an excellent leadership lesson for all of us.

I attended a Navy training school prior to reporting to my new duty station as the second-in-command, or Executive Officer (XO), of a ship. I'll never forget one of the instructors reminding us that an important part of our next job was to make the Commanding Officer (CO) successful. Although most of us had over 10 years of experience, it was time to "check your ego" at the door. As an XO, I needed to carry out the vision and goals of the CO and maintain high standards each day to enable the command as a whole to perform with excellence. Loyalty plus integrity should guide a good XO. Just as with Joshua, I and other XOs needed to be patient until we earned the opportunity at the right time in the future to serve as Commanding Officer.

hearkening back to his own experience as a young man staying close to the tent. The honest display of the flaws and sins of the people of the Bible attests to the credibility of this holy book. But Joshua—a military man to the core—is honored as a good guy.

If you've ever questioned whether a person who has fought, killed, and conquered could be considered a true "good guy," here is your answer in Joshua.

At the age of 110, Joshua finished his earthly service by calling the people to wholeheartedly follow God and by stating again his own unwavering commitment to live for God.

"Now fear the LORD and serve him with all faithfulness. Throw away the gods your ancestors worshiped beyond the Euphrates River and in Egypt, and serve the LORD. But if serving the LORD seems undesirable to you, then choose for yourselves this day whom you will serve . . . But as for me and my household, we will serve the LORD" (Joshua 24:14–15).

RECAP

While military activity in the Bible and throughout history includes both good and evil, the purpose for which many have served in the military is that they might be part of a force for good in the world. This is important to grasp as we move forward, because God calls each Christian to be a spiritual warrior.

> It was not by their sword that they won the land, nor did their arm bring them victory; it was your right hand, your arm, and the light of your face, for you loved them.
> **PSALM 44:3**

CHAPTER 3

People Group

THE MILITARY IS a special people group, set apart and unique. I have seen this over and over in relating to military people through the years: Sailors, Soldiers, Airmen, Marines, Guardians, and Coast Guardsmen often have what I call a "military heart." For most, their military heart does not mean they are angry, vengeful, or eager to fight. Instead, it means there is something about their military heart that is noble, self-sacrificing, protective, courageous, and instinctively understanding of the big picture of what is at stake. Admiral Kemp says, "This means willingly carrying out expectations and responsibilities due to a moral conviction—to do the right thing in the right way at the right time." Often, there is a tenderness there as well. Military spouses are also a special people group whom I honor. They hold down the fort during military deployments, provide consistent care for the children, make the best of multiple moves, and maintain a stable home environment while also being a safe person for their spouse. They are heroes in their own right.

Let us consider how this unique people group characteristic is displayed by a few more military leaders and movements in the Bible.

DEBORAH

We meet Deborah in the unhinged pages of the Bible book of Judges which chronicles between 300 to 400 years of Israel's erratic history between the time of Joshua and Samuel.[1] Deborah is the fourth judge in a lineup of 13, with Samuel being both the last judge and the first of what are called the prophets.[2] While not filling a military position, her military-related leadership experience is significant to the scriptural Story.

We understandably equate the term "judge" with what we understand a judge is in English—one who determines and dispenses justice. Deborah was such a judge. She handled disputes between the people as she held court under a palm tree (Judges 4:5).

But Deborah, as the other Old Testament judges of that day, had responsibilities that encompassed much more. Though not trained as

---

[1] A later chronology places the span of the judges at around 300 years. See *NLT Illustrated Study Bible* p. 446–450.
[2] Deborah would be 5th of 14 if we include Moses as the first judge. See Exodus 18:13–27.

THE ADMIRAL'S CORNER

Tribal Uniqueness

Once, when I attended a meeting of all Navy Flag Officers with the Chief of Naval Operations, as part of his remarks he reminded us that the Navy is a "tribal organization" (this would apply to the other Services as well). He said we are a unique culture with unique traditions. We have a unique appearance (uniforms, haircuts). We have a unique way of speaking (military lingo, unique acronyms). We have a unique way of doing things. We have a unique code of conduct. We train our young to learn our tribal ways in order to assume greater responsibilities in the tribe. And we preserve and promote our unique culture by telling "stories" unique to our tribe. In the Navy, we would call these "sea stories," both historical and current stories about our tribe to help ingrain a sense of why it is special to be part of this tribe.

military personnel by profession, their leadership sometimes included being a military leader (much like a country's president). God raised up judges as deliverers to help get his people back on track after they had done the opposite of what Moses and Joshua had commanded them to do. In the book of Judges, the nation went through seven cycles of sin, oppression, repentance, and deliverance. Deborah's 40 years as judge served as the high point of a very troubled 300+ years.

Deborah was also a prophet and the leader of Israel. She is connected to Lappidoth—which to some scholars is the name of her husband (not a common name) and to others a description of her as a fiery woman ("lappid" can be translated "torches").[3] Deborah's leadership specifically emerged and was carried out from her embodied femininity: "I, Deborah, arose a mother in Israel" (Judges 5:7).

In the battle account that unfolds for us in Judges 4 and the recap in the song of chapter 5, we are told that Deborah went out to a battle at the insistence of the military commander, Barak. He recognized her God-given authority as well as her strategic significance for overseeing the battle. As far as I can tell, we do not see Deborah involved in the actual fighting.[4] Nevertheless, she delivered the mission orders as well as the pre-battle encouragement to Barak and the troops, "This is the day the LORD has given Sisera into your hands. Has not the LORD gone ahead of you?" (Judges 4:14).

The enemies the Israelites were against in this battle were the Canaanites, whose commander, Sisera, had cruelly oppressed Israel for 20 years. Their advanced military was well-armed and known for its fast iron chariots. Canaanites were also known for their detestable pagan religious practices which included ritual sexual abuse, brutality, and burning of their own children as sacrifices to idols.[5]

I believe there is much meaning to the phrase Deborah declares, "I, Deborah, arose a mother in Israel." Scripture gives us the image of a "mama bear" in describing the fierce love one has for her children and the lengths

---

3 Marg Mowczko, "What's in a Name?", margmowczko.com.
4 Note: this passage is not about the ethics of women in combat, and to read that subject into these verses could show this passage to evidence support for both sides.
5 That the World May Know, "Fertility Cults of Canaan."

to which she will go to protect them.[6] It is a term that means, "Don't mess with me and my kids or you will be so sorry!" Deborah was like a mother bear who would do all she could to keep the evil practices of the Canaanites away from her beloved people.

Not only was Deborah a fierce protector as she led Israel, but we see that another woman, Jael, had the final say in the defeat of Sisera and his army. Remember the Bible is not rated PG as you read Jael's genius and courageous take-down of Sisera in Judges 4:17–24.

GIDEON

The judge who followed Deborah was a man named Gideon. He led the Israelites out of seven years of oppression by the Midianites who "ravaged the land," leaving the people of God impoverished (See Judges 6:1–6). Take a look at Gideon, because he is not who we might consider a typical military person, yet he became a great military leader. As we think about the unique people group of the military, I believe he represents many current service members whom we would be wise to not stereotype.

Gideon was a farmer, threshing wheat in a winepress to hide it from the Midianites, when the angel of the LORD sat down under an oak tree nearby. The angel greeted him with, "The LORD is with you, mighty warrior." And the first words out of Gideon's mouth were, "but Sir" (or "Pardon me, my lord"). Gideon didn't fall down, didn't worship, didn't revel in the fact that the angel of the LORD was sitting under his tree and speaking highly of him. Instead, Gideon questioned. He already assumed that the Lord had abandoned his people, and Gideon vented his frustration and anger. While we might not initially describe Gideon as noble, we see right away that he is honest—honest about his doubts, his fears, his concerns, and his inadequacies. He was not rebuked for this transparency.

Then the angel, specifically called "the LORD," replied to Gideon, "Go in the strength you have and save Israel out of Midian's hand. Am I not sending you?" (Judges 6:14).[7]

---

6 See 2 Samuel 17:8, Proverbs 17:12.
7 Biblical scholars debate whether this is a "Christophany," meaning an Old Testament appearance of Christ. What is clear is that this angel is an emissary with authority from God.

THE ADMIRAL'S CORNER

OPDEC

Operational Deception (OPDEC) is a military strategy to mislead, confuse, and deceive the enemy by causing them to "see" something that is not reality, thereby providing a military advantage for one's own forces. Gideon demonstrated the finest in OPDEC during his confrontation with the Midianite forces, who vastly outnumbered his forces—over 100,000 to Gideon's 300.

First, he timed his attack to take place just after the "guard" had been changed at midnight. Military leaders know this is time of higher vulnerability—it's the middle of the night. Sleepy new sentries who have likely just been awakened are taking over guard duties without the benefit of having acquired full awareness of the surrounding situation.

Then, coupled with excellent timing in the pitch black of night, Gideon gave each of his 300 warriors a horn and a hidden lantern, and they surrounded the huge Midianite camp on all sides with their meager forces. Upon signal and in unison, each of Gideon's men broke the clay jars hiding the lanterns, blew their horns, and screamed battle cries from all directions. Mostly asleep, the Midianites awoke in terror to the confounding sight and noise, and utter mayhem broke loose. Most of the Midianites confused each other for the enemy and killed their fellow warriors, while others fled in panic. With God's help and a masterful OPDEC plan, Gideon and the Israelites were totally victorious.

The next words out of Gideon's mouth were . . . you guessed it . . . "but Lord . . ." He went on to question, "How can I save Israel? My clan is the weakest in Manasseh, and I am the least in my family" (Judges 6:15).

After the angel showed God's power and confirmed his identity by bringing fire from a rock, Gideon realized he was dealing with The. Sovereign. Lord. and feared for his life. The LORD said, "Peace! Do not be afraid. You are not going to die."[8] Then Gideon built an altar to God and named it Yahweh Shalom—"The LORD is Peace."

The story of Gideon continues through Judges chapters 6–8. Much more could be said about this military man. What I want to highlight here is two-fold. First, not all military leaders fit the stereotype of risk-taking and driven justice-seekers, nor have some aspired to their leadership positions. That does not mean they are not called and equipped to serve and to lead. Secondly, before Gideon became a successful military leader, he deeply understood the fact that "the LORD is Peace." Peace-making is a very real and legitimate driving force in the hearts of many in this people group of the military.

IDENTITY AND INSTRUCTIONS FOR A PEOPLE GROUP

A whole chapter of the Bible, Deuteronomy 20, is devoted to God's instructions to the military when they go to war. These specifications include:

- Offer peace first.
- What to do when you are afraid—and it's not just "don't be afraid." It's more.
- Don't cut down the trees when you conquer land or practice a scorched earth policy (a practice commonly held by surrounding pagan nations). "Are the trees of the field people, that you should besiege them?" (Deuteronomy 20:19b).
- Understand why some places and people must be destroyed. God is serious about his people worshiping him alone. Keep in mind that this is in the context of offering peace first. Throughout the

---

8 LORD capitalized in Scripture refers to the Hebrew word Yahweh. The caps used here in the text could also be an Old Testament reference to the deity of Jesus Christ.

rest of Scripture, we see people from these enemy nations living alongside the people of God (See also Deuteronomy 12:29-31). This is not ethnic cleansing nor genocide.[9]
- Rely on God's presence with you in war.

In Numbers Chapter 1, instructions for a draft are set out, including a religious exemption for the tribe of Levi. Did you know that the draft goes back to at least 1445 B.C.?[10] Though sometimes Bible chapters like Numbers 1 can seem tedious and even boring, there is a glory to the care that God takes with his people—with their lifestyle, their systems, and their worship. God is not haphazard in his leadership. He wants his people to represent to the rest of the world an orderly, respectful, loving, and vibrant community. Tedious—at times; beautiful—always.

God calls all his followers to be a special *people group* who are known for loving God and loving people.[11] Jesus could not be clearer in Mark 12:29-31 as he quotes Deuteronomy 6:4-5.

> "The most important one [command]," answered Jesus, "is this: 'Hear, O Israel: The LORD our God, the LORD is one. Love the LORD your God with all your heart and with all your soul and with all your mind and with all your strength.' The second is this: 'Love your neighbor as yourself.' There is no commandment greater than these.

Consider also Colossians 3:12, "Therefore, as God's chosen people, holy and dearly loved, clothe yourselves with compassion, kindness, humility, gentleness and patience." And 1 Peter 2:9-10 says, "But you are a chosen people, a royal priesthood, a holy nation, God's special possession, that you may declare the praises of him who called you out of darkness into his wonderful light. Once you were not a people, but now you are the people of God; once you had not received mercy, but now you have received mercy."

---

9 See chapters 8 and 12 of *Bloody, Brutal, and Barbaric?*
10 NLT Study Bible, A19 referring to Israel's draft.
11 See Deuteronomy 10:12-22.

RECAP

The military is a people group set apart for specific influence and impact. God himself gave directions to the military of Israel in the Bible. Furthermore, he gave specific examples of godly military leadership through Deborah and Gideon.

How important is it to us that the people of God are, like the military, set apart? What influence and impact could we as Christians and spiritual warriors have if we were more serious about our specific identity? We will think about this more.

CHAPTER 4

Professional

THE MILITARY IS made up of professionals. They are trained, skilled, and in continual mission-readiness. They do not shirk their duties. They must not shirk their duties.

What a gift to the world these professionals are. Each one has been given tasks to which they are uniquely suited and trained, having gone through a battery of tests for aptitude and accomplishments. Each one is expected to stay physically fit. All have the opportunity to advance in rank based on their performance in their job, their degree of being a team player, and their demonstrated leadership. They function as an organized system where each person and unit critically depends on the proficiency of the other.

Our Airman friend, Technical Sergeant Kyle Carnegie, is a TMDE Tech Section Chief at the PMEL, which translated from Military to English is Test Measurement Diagnostic Equipment Technician at the Precision Measurement Equipment Laboratory. (I'm not sure if the English is more understandable!)

Kyle describes his job in this way: "My primary job is to direct, equip, and train two dozen or so airmen in my section to ensure that quality calibrations of test measurement and diagnostic equipment (TMDE) go out to our various military customers in a timely manner. They must also be traceable to the National Institute of Standards and Technology (NIST), internationally agreed standards (meaning there is a trail of measurements

THE ADMIRAL'S CORNER

Handling Power

We can learn just as much from reflecting on mistakes as from reviewing successes. When I was attending a required Navy training course prior to reporting to my first ship command, during the lunch period, I'd often review the ship "accident" files that the school maintained—mostly ship groundings and collisions. Typically, there were many small mistakes made that combined to result in the major casualty. These were invaluable lessons for me later to strive not to repeat.

And so, there is great value in learning from an Old Testament military leader whose life might be summarized as "the rise and fall of King Saul." Saul's story is recorded in the Book of 1 Samuel. Saul was placed by God as Israel's first king although Saul saw himself as unworthy. The prophet Samuel both anointed Saul and was God's key advisor to King Saul.

Initially humble, Saul asked for and depended on God's guidance, and as he achieved great battle successes, he honored God for his victories. But with additional victories, the temptations of power took root and he came to believe his success was due to his own talents. For each of us, no matter our position, we are always accountable to someone, and especially to God. In his growing selfishness, King Saul became impatient and didn't wait for his chief advisor, Samuel, as he was instructed (See Proverbs 15:22). Then in 1 Samuel 15, Saul failed to carry out God's orders specifically, and then built a monument to himself after a victory over the Amalekites. He forgot to Whom he owed his victories.

His growing obsession with power was further evidenced when rather than celebrate when one of his key commanders (David) began achieving great military victories, Saul became jealous to the point of plotting David's demise. This is a reminder that when a military commander is achieving the larger mission, that leader should not care who gets the credit. Worldly power corrupted King Saul when he chose to ignore where his real power came from: the Commander of Heaven's Armies.

from the highest standards all the way to the user's equipment). We are in essence a quality assurance on measurement equipment, ensuring that it measures safely, accurately, reliably and traceably.

"We take Air Force equipment which ranges from torque wrenches and pressure gauges to oscilloscopes, multimeters, and specialized aircraft test sets. We check all the functions that are used in these against a standard. If the item is accurate within the tolerance allowed for its job, then we certify its quality. If it fails and we can't fix the issue, then we tag it for repair by a specialist at depot maintenance or mark it as condemned and it is recycled or disposed of."[1]

Sergeant Carnegie's job is performed day after day away from the limelight in an independent facility with a clean climate-controlled workspace (73 degrees Fahrenheit +/-6 degrees). The workspace is behind an airlock, and personnel are required to clean their boots prior to entering to try to keep dust and dirt out. Kyle's military service takes place mostly behind the scenes. Yet he knows his work is vital to the success of a mission. As he puts it, "We calibrate the test sets used to ensure the pilot can trust their controls even when they can't see around them because of conditions like inclement weather. You can imagine the disaster if any one of those gauges is faulty, and if the test set is faulty, it might affect multiple aircraft causing them all to read erroneously. We don't think about the fuel gauge on our car requiring calibration because if it is off, the worst we probably have to deal with is an embarrassing hike to the gas station. But on an aircraft, that's the difference between life and death."

In Scripture we are given examples of military people as professionals. Notice these descriptors of expertise:

- Judges 20:16–17 details troops who are "fit for battle," including 700 who were left-handed, "each of whom could sling a stone at a hair and not miss."
- In 2 Samuel 17:8 David is described as "an experienced fighter."
- In 2 Kings 5 we read of military leader Naaman, a "valiant soldier."

---

1 I am quoting TSgt Carnegie with his permission from written conversations via email and messaging in 2016, 2020, and 2024.

- King Uzziah in 2 Chronicles 26 has a well-trained and well-armed army.
- In Luke 7, we hear of a Centurion who is both a competent and caring leader.

Let's consider another Old Testament military professional—one of the most influential people of the Bible—David.

DAVID

David from Bethlehem was a great military commander and the king over Israel from 1011 to 971 BC. He was called a "brave man and a warrior" who "speaks well and is fine-looking," "an experienced fighter," and a "man after God's own heart."[2]

Teen-age David's first battle with a person (he had already killed a lion and a bear) was the widely celebrated story of David and Goliath found in 1 Samuel 17. The youngest of eight sons, David was responsible for the care of the family's sheep before he was enlisted by King Saul to play a harp as music therapy and be an armor bearer. He was going back and forth from Saul's employ to home and shepherding, then to the front lines of battle with supplies (including cheese!) where his older brothers and the Israelite soldiers faced the enemy of the Philistines.

It was after forty days of Goliath's taunts to the Israelites that David took action. He asked, "Who is this uncircumcised Philistine that he should defy the armies of the living God?" (1 Samuel 17:26b). And although his brother accused David of being conceited, David went to King Saul and volunteered to fight the giant warrior.

David was an expert with the sling, his weapon of choice. He took five smooth stream stones, ran toward the battle line and felled Goliath with his first stone which sank into the enemy's forehead. Then he cut off Goliath's head with Goliath's sword.

David advanced in rank in the Israelite army, but it was not long before King Saul became jealous of David and his sudden popularity with the

---

2 See 1 Samuel 13:14, 1 Samuel 16:18, 2 Samuel 17:8–10, Acts 13:22.

people of Israel. I do not see an indication here that Saul knew of Samuel's earlier anointing of David as the next king. Still, Saul was threatened by David, tried to kill him, and ultimately sent him away.[3]

Many of the poems, songs, and psalms in the book of Psalms were written by David. In these we hear his shepherd's heart, his warrior's heart, and his leader's heart. We also experience the inner fire that drove him to run toward the battle when the name and the glory of God Almighty was dishonored.

---

3 See 1 Samuel 16, 18–20.

THE ADMIRAL'S CORNER

Special Forces

Although he didn't jump out of airplanes or conduct underwater raids, David epitomized the strategic value of Special Forces operations. Chased for many years by King Saul, David knew he needed a small and highly mobile unit of warriors. They lived off the land in the wilderness, among the hills, and in caves. They changed locations frequently, knowing that they were being watched by others who might report their whereabouts back to Saul.

David used stealth, conducting reconnaissance (RECON) into the enemy's camp at night (1 Samuel 26), while at other times avoiding direct battles where they would be at a military disadvantage. His men conducted an impressive rescue operation, saving the town of Keilah from oppressors (1 Samuel 23). David even employed what we might call PSYOPS, or Psychological Operations, when he and his men "joined" the Philistine army under king Achish as a survival tactic to avoid Saul's pursuit (1 Samuel 29). The ruse was very convincing, while also allowing David to conduct "unconventional warfare" against other enemies of Israel without Achish noticing. Impressive. Perhaps we should make David an honorary Green Beret or SEAL.

David was a shepherd, son, husband, father, brother, musician, friend, author, and military hero. His story included significant moral failure, sin, and repentance—also heartbreak, loss, and redemption. David's life is perhaps summed up well in his own words from Psalm 18:1–3.

> I love you, O LORD, my strength. The LORD is my rock, my fortress and my deliverer; my God is my rock, in whom I take refuge. He is my shield and the horn of my salvation, my stronghold. I call to the LORD, who is worthy of praise, and I am saved from my enemies.

From David's line, another King born in Bethlehem would arise. A thousand years later, Messiah Jesus came to earth, fulfilling prophecies made by David and others.[4] He wasn't a "professional" conquering king like the people had pictured. But he was indeed the King of kings and Lord of Lords.

CRITICAL CIVILIANS

Abigail

Sometimes overlooked are battles fought without violence, won with words and acts of kindness, and by professionals who are experts in negotiation. Effective militaries are typically enhanced by critical civilian "support forces." The Bible includes these stories too.

Connected to the warrior story of David is the resourceful story of Abigail, a woman described in 1 Samuel 25:3 as "intelligent and beautiful." Unfortunately, her husband Nabal, though very wealthy, was "surly and mean in his dealings." At the time of this account, David was leading a ragtag army of about 600 men (see 1 Samuel 22:1–2, 23:13). He and his troops had previously protected the shepherds of Nabal and their flocks over a stretch of time. When David sent messengers to ask Nabal for hospitality as compensation, Nabal's response was an "absolutely not" filled with insulting denigration that categorized David as a slave and his troops as nobodies.

---

4 Psalm 110, Mark 12:35–37.

David's swift response was meant to answer insult with violence, as he and four hundred of his men prepared their swords and headed for Nabal's community planning to kill all the men. An attentive servant alerted Abigail and she acted quickly. In 1 Samuel 25:14–35 we hear the details of Abigail's intelligent, courageous, and humble apology as well as her generous hospitality. Further, as she "saves the day" she also points David to his highest responsibilities—to the Lord his God and to the calling God placed on his life when he was anointed by Samuel to be the future king.

Wise Woman on the Wall

In the bloody chapter of 2 Samuel 20 we meet another civilian who also alters the course of a military effort. We do not know her name, only that she was a "wise woman" (2 Samuel 20:14–22). A siege is laid against the city of Abel in an attempt to extract an enemy troublemaker named Sheba. The wise woman yells from the city wall, asking to speak to Joab, the military commander. She then chastises him for overreacting in trying to destroy a city that had been a bastion of wisdom in the country for many years. She asks what he really wants. When he tells her, she advises the people of the city to deliver, and widespread destruction is averted.

Words can be powerful; courage can be convincing. In the last two examples we also see women who did not let their cultural limitations keep them from battling for the good of others in whatever ways they could.

RECAP

The security of a nation and the safety of its people are often greatly influenced by the professionalism and integrity of its military. The responsibility on all soldiers is heavy; their ability to work with excellence has long-range ramifications. Further, some battles are best fought with shrewd and insightful words and good deeds.

We as Christians would do well to consider the weight and scope of our responsibilities in the Kingdom of God and to grow in our development and practice of personal integrity and spiritual competence.

CHAPTER 5

Positioned

THE MILITARY IS strategically positioned and placed. Throughout Scripture and to this day, God in His wisdom has not only allowed, but also caused military people to occupy spaces where few others have ever been, thus trusting them with the possibility of tremendous influence in ways most of us could only dream about.

Think about it. Military people stand next to presidents, kings, and queens. Military people enter countries where no missionaries are allowed. Whatever happens in countries, kingdoms, and the world in the years to come, the military will be part of it.

The inauguration of the President and Vice President of the United States in 2021 was carried out during a world-wide pandemic. The crowds that usually gathered at an inauguration were replaced by flags. However, one group of people was very visible and active in several facets of the ceremony: the military. Military members provided security for the event, instrumental music and accompaniment, and in the tradition of this country, they also escorted the new president to the White House.[1]

More profound is the historical example of Allied Forces witnessing the atrocities of concentration camps as they were the first to enter at the end of World War II. Journalist Dave Roos writes, "For many soldiers,

---

[1] Lopez, "Despite COVID-19 Restrictions, Service Members Play Important Role in Inauguration."

seeing Dachau for themselves gave the war a new meaning. They weren't just fighting an enemy; they were fighting evil itself."[2]

Here is a sample of strategic positions military people occupied in the narrative of the Bible, some of which will be discussed further in this chapter:

- Soldiers were the first of God's people to enter the Promised Land (Joshua).
- David's fighting men stayed close to him as king (1 Chronicles 12).
- A Centurion was the example Jesus gave the people of one with "great faith" (Matthew 8 and Luke 7).
- Soldiers were right beside Jesus the entire way to the cross.
- Soldiers were at the tomb when Jesus rose from the dead.
- A Roman captain was one of two doorways of the gospel to the Gentiles in Acts 10. (The other was the Samaritan woman in John 4.)
- A soldier stayed with Paul for two years while he was under house arrest (Acts 28:16 and 30–31). I wonder how many of Paul's military guards were also introduced to Jesus Christ in those years.

Let us now go deeper into some of the military stories from the New Testament as we consider the characteristic of "positioned."

MUSIC TO WELCOME THE KING

As a reminder, the Bible is divided into two main sections, the Old Testament and the New Testament. The Old Testament occurs and was written before Christ's time on earth (noted as BC—Before Christ, or BCE—Before the Common Era). The New Testament begins with the Genealogy of Jesus Christ and his birth, between 6 and 4 BC, and tells us of the life and teachings of Jesus and the life and teachings of his people in the first century AD (for Anno Domini—the year of our Lord, or CE—Common Era).[3]

---

2 "The Horrifying Discovery of Dachau Concentration Camp—And Its Liberation by US Troops."
3 Logos Press, "Can We Know What Year Jesus Was Born?"

Similar to the early appearance of heavenly military at the beginning of the Old Testament (the warrior angel stationed at the entrance of Eden), the New Testament is heralded in with an army of angels. But this time they come in celebration rather than in judgment.

In Luke 2:13-14 an angel brings the news of the birth of Messiah to shepherds in a field on the night of Jesus' birthday. The angel is joined by "a vast host of others—the armies of heaven—praising God and saying, 'Glory to God in highest heaven, and peace on earth to those with whom God is pleased.'"[4]

Could it be that it is an extra powerful experience when military and music are combined? One of our military friends, SFC Emily "MJ" McAleesejergins, is a vocalist for the West Point Band. I remember watching and listening to a video of MJ and the Army band performing for a West Point Commencement and the President. While her voice was stunning, her presence as a soldier added another layer of meaning to her beautiful rendition of the national anthem and to the joy of the troops listening.

The most spectacular combination of military and music occurred on the night Jesus was born. And let us not miss the message from this heavenly military choir: "Peace on earth!"

A WICKED COMMANDER

Tragically, the first encounter we have in the New Testament with human military troops is in Matthew 2:13-18 when the wicked King Herod orders the murder of baby boys in Bethlehem in his rash determination to kill any potential threat to his throne.[5] Sometimes the reality of military being "positioned" results in being forced to witness or participate in atrocities.

This passage brings up the challenging subject of carrying out orders or missions that result in ethical dilemmas for military members. They have taken an oath to obey lawful orders. But what if innocent civilians die because of the aerial bombing of a high-priority military target? Or how does one respond to the youth who is about to throw a hand grenade at a platoon of soldiers? I am compelled to pray for military people who have

---

4 From the New Living Translation (NLT).
5 It is assumed, but not explicitly stated in Scripture, that soldiers were used to carry out this order.

THE ADMIRAL'S CORNER

Carrying out Orders
In the New Testament, when it came to carrying out orders, the soldiers under King Herod or Pontius Pilate did not have much choice. Either they carried out their orders no matter how brutal, or they would often be killed. Godly justice and morality were not considerations. As we look throughout history, this is not uncommon in power-oriented authoritarian societies. In the U.S. military, we have learned some hard lessons from some leaders' mistakes over the years. But due to our current training of military leaders, coupled with the "laws of war," I believe it is rare for our leaders to give unjust orders. Additionally, each member of the U.S. military is trained that they have the right to refuse to carry out orders that are illegal or immoral.

---

been put in such difficult situations, including those who consequently suffer with Post Traumatic Stress or Moral Injury. May the Lord heal, comfort, and show mercy to these individuals.

POSITION AND POWER

The characteristic of "positioned" highlights the importance of the appropriate use of power. In Luke 3:7–18 we read of John the Baptist warning a crowd to repent. There were soldiers in the crowd who asked what repentance would look like for them. John replied, "Don't extort money and don't accuse people falsely—be content with your pay." As Dr. Esau McCaulley says, John was speaking to "the personal responsibility and integrity of the officers themselves. He calls upon those with power to use that power to uphold the inherent dignity of all residents and to never use that power for their own ends."[6] Military members, who are all trained to be leaders, must not abuse their authority.

---

6   Esau McCaulley, *Reading While Black*, p. 45. Quoted with permission from the author.

A RIGHTEOUS COMMANDER

The next time we meet the military in the New Testament is in the beautiful story of the Centurion of Great Faith, recorded in Matthew 8:5–13 and Luke 7:1–10. A centurion was a Roman commander of 80–100 soldiers. While we are not told this centurion's name, we learn much about his character in these few verses.

He was a leader, a patriot, one who loved people, and a Gentile (non-Jew) who was actively involved in building a synagogue for the Jews in the area under his jurisdiction. He understood both the power and responsibility of authority. He used his position and leadership privileges well.

In a historical era where servants were part of many household structures and often regarded as "less than," this officer valued his servants; he cared for them. And one of his servants was terminally ill. When the centurion heard that Jesus was in town, he sent some Jewish elders to plead on his behalf for Jesus to heal his servant.

Three words say so much: three words from the centurion and three words from Jesus.

"Say the word." The centurion believed that Jesus possessed genuine authority, and that he only needed to speak healing and his servant would be healed. As a commander, he understood the power of words from one in charge. And he knew Jesus was in charge.

"Such great faith." Jesus responded not only to the centurion and his friends who had been relaying his messages to Jesus, but also to all those following him. "I tell you the truth, I have not found anyone in Israel with such great faith" (Matthew 8:10b).

A military man, a Roman officer, and a Gentile—this centurion is the one Jesus holds up to all of us as an example of "such great faith." What would it look like for us to follow the centurion's example? I think it might have something to do with our understanding of and belief in Jesus, exemplified by "say the word."

AT THE CROSS

Throughout Jesus' ministry, the Roman military had a place as part of the general social structure. However, we don't come face to face with them again like we do in the verses that detail the crucifixion of Jesus, recounted in Matthew 27:27-66, Mark 15, Luke 22:63-23:49, and John 19.

Much could be said about the strategic positions of military people in significant historic events. For now, let us acknowledge that it was soldiers who beat Jesus, soldiers who made him a crown of thorns, soldiers who mocked and tortured him, soldiers who cast lots for his clothing, and soldiers who drove the nails into his hands and feet.

This was not the first crucifixion in which these soldiers participated. But this was the only crucifixion that would change the world forever.

Jesus had his own army of angels at the ready. But he chose to submit himself to an unjust trial motivated by envy, a cruel crucifixion carried out by occupying troops, and the undeserved punishment for sin he did not commit so that humankind whom he loved might be redeemed.[7]

At least one soldier—another centurion, along with a few of his troops who stood near the cross as Jesus died—realized Who was on that cross and perhaps some of what was really happening. "This soldier looked beyond what 'soldiers do' and looked at God Himself."[8]

For three hours the sky turned dark in the middle of the day. The earth shook. Rocks split and tombs broke open as godly people of the past were raised to life. The heavy curtain to the Holy of Holies in the temple was torn in half from top to bottom as Jesus took his last breath. Only God could split that curtain in that way.

Roman soldiers were all around while these events took place. Jewish people who had come to Jerusalem for the Passover filled the area. Religious leaders were likely nearby, believing they had finally eliminated the threat to their societal control. The apostle John and several women who were Jesus' close followers, including his mother Mary, stood in the vicinity of the cross.

But those closest to the wooden cross—closest to Jesus in His dark hours of suffering, close enough to be able to actually touch him—were soldiers. And it was these soldiers, and their centurion leader, who were the first to declare the identity of the Messiah after he sacrificed himself for the sins of the world: "Surely, this was the Son of God" (Matthew 27:54,

---

7 See Matthew 26:53; Matthew 27:18 NASB; Isaiah 53:5; Romans 5:6-11; and Romans 8:1-4.
8 Jerri Kayll, Cadence International.

Mark 15:39).[9] Strategically positioned soldiers offered one of the most profound pronouncements of all time.

Each of us now has the opportunity to come near to this cross. The blood sacrifice made by Jesus is available to each of us as the once-for-all payment for our wrongdoings. The honor of the innocent Son of God is offered us as a gift that wipes away all our sin and shame.

With which soldiers will we align our response? The ones who mocked and scorned, or the ones who realized and declared the true identity of Jesus?

We would be remiss if we did not also note that it was Roman soldiers who guarded Jesus' tomb, soldiers who saw an angel as Jesus was resurrected— "and they shook and became like dead men" (Matthew 28:4)— and soldiers who were paid by the religious leaders to spread the lie that the disciples stole the body of Jesus from the tomb.

THE OPEN DOOR TO THE GOSPEL

In all branches of the military, there is a ladder of promotion in rank. In the book of Acts, written by a doctor and follower of Jesus named Luke (also the author of the Gospel of Luke), we meet Cornelius, a military man who had advanced as far as a centurion of the Italian Regiment. New Testament scholar Dr. Craig Keener says the regiment's name, "simply indicates that the cohort's original members were Italians."[10] This group of soldiers likely included many who were of Syrian birth, and it was part of the five regiments, or cohorts of up to 600 men each, stationed in Caesarea at that time.

Luke begins the story of Cornelius in Acts 10 with an honoring description: "He and all his family were devout and God-fearing; he gave generously to those in need and prayed to God regularly" (Acts 10:2). The Greek word *oikos*, translated "family" in the NIV Bible can also be understood as "household," including servants. Dr. Keener notes that many soldiers did not get married until they retired after 20 years of service.[11]

---

9   Luke 23:47 says, "Surely this was a righteous [innocent] man."
10 Craig Keener and InterVarsity Press, *The IVP Bible Background Commentary*, 349.
11 Keener and InterVarsity Press, 350.

During one of his regular prayer times, an angel visited Centurion Cornelius in a vision—a very real encounter, not a dream—and told him that God had heard his prayers and that Cornelius was to send men to Joppa to fetch the Apostle Peter and bring him back.

Meanwhile, the next day, Peter was on his roof in prayer and received what to him was a very disturbing vision. Three times he was shown something like a sheet full of animals Jews were forbidden to eat and he was told to kill and eat them. Peter's first response was basically, "No way!"

But the Lord spoke to Peter, "Do not call anything impure that God has made clean."[12] And just then some visitors showed up at his door. The Holy Spirit told Peter to go with these visitors and the next day they headed back to Caesarea to the home of Cornelius.

Peter was warmly (albeit too warmly—see Acts 10:25-26) welcomed in the house full of Cornelius' relatives and friends. There Peter and Cornelius related their corresponding vision stories and Peter began to explain the gospel of Christ to the full house. The people listened and responded in faith. The Holy Spirit came upon them and the new believers were baptized.

> I now realize how true it is that God does not show favoritism but accepts from every nation the one who fears him and does what is right. You know the message God sent to the people of Israel, announcing the good news of peace through Jesus Christ, who is Lord of all.
> —Acts 10:34-36

Some of the Jewish Christians, upon hearing what happened at Cornelius' house, criticized and questioned Peter. So, the story was recounted again in Acts 11 as Peter gave them an explanation. The result was, "When the others heard this, they stopped objecting and began praising God. They said, 'We can see that God has also given the Gentiles the privilege of repenting of their sins and receiving eternal life'" (Acts 11:18 NLT).

---

12 See Acts 10:15.

Just like that, the door to the gospel, the good news of salvation, was permanently opened wide—not only for the Jews, but also for the Gentiles (every nationality besides the Jews).[13] Peace through Jesus Christ was, and is, available to all who believe in Him.

And which human held that door open? A military man, Centurion Cornelius.

RECAP

Because of their unique responsibilities, military people are strategically positioned and thus have the opportunity to be highly influential in the lives of leaders and in the events of world history.

As Christians, we also get to choose how we handle the stewardship of our place, position, responsibilities, and influence. May it be in a way that honors Christ the King.

---

13 As noted previously, Jesus first opened the door to the Gentiles through the Samaritan women in John 4. However, the early Christian church as a whole did not understand this until Acts 11.

CHAPTER 6

Portrayal

MILITARY PEOPLE CAN give us an earthly portrayal of God the warrior and his battle tactics in the unseen realm. They can also give Christians a picture of how we are to engage in spiritual warfare. In this chapter, we will focus on the warrior heart and activity of God. Keep in mind that nothing about God's battle involvement will ever violate his flawless love, justice, mercy, integrity, righteousness, wisdom, and goodness.

GOD IS A WARRIOR

In the Bible God gives us images of who he is. These portrayals do not describe the totality or comprehensive nature of God, but they help us understand God's character in human terms and relate to him accordingly. They tell us not only who he is, but something about who we are. For example, God is a shepherd, parent, creator, artist, and king. Thus, we can know that we are loved and protected, made with care, and our authority is limited.

God also tells us he is the God of Heaven's Armies (Psalm 89:6–8 NLT). His heavenly hosts of angels are not only "ministering spirits sent to serve those who will inherit salvation" (Hebrews 1:14), but an organized military.[1] God's enemies are both heavenly and human—the devil and his dark angels (demons) and unrepentant people who persist in wickedness.[2]

Here are some passages that describe God's military presence:

> For the Lord your God is the one who goes with you to fight for you against your enemies to give you victory.
> —Deuteronomy 20:4

> The Lord has opened his arsenal and brought out the weapons of his wrath, for the Sovereign Lord Almighty has work to do in the land of the Babylonians.
> —Jeremiah 50:25

> I have commanded those I prepared for battle;
>   I have summoned my warriors to carry out my wrath—
>   those who rejoice in my triumph.
> —Isaiah 13:3

> The Lord thunders
>   at the head of his army;
> his forces are beyond number,
>   and mighty is the army that obeys his command.
> The day of the Lord is great;
>   it is dreadful.
>   Who can endure it?
> —Joel 2:11

Do you sense the intensity of these verses? Are they a bit frightening, or perhaps even comforting? I sense both—I feel it in my gut—they are ominous and awe-inspiring. The ramifications of God's military activity are more than my mind can handle. But I must not turn away; I seek to better understand. This is the God I know and worship and want to know

---

[1] I have found the book *Angels Elect & Evil*, by C. Fred Dickason an excellent resource on this topic.
[2] Consider these examples: Genesis 6; Deuteronomy 9:4–5; 2 Chronicles 7:14; Psalm 1 and 37; Matthew 13:49–50; Luke 10:18; Romans 5:10; 2 Thessalonians 1:5–10; and Revelation 12:9.

more. Although it may challenge our sense of logic, God is both the Prince of Peace (Isaiah 9:6; Romans 15:33) as well as the Mighty Warrior.

YAHWEH TSEBAOTH

I was introduced to the *Names of God Bible* (NOG) by my sister-in-law, Connie, who had my name in a family Christmas gift exchange. At the beginning of each book of the Old Testament, the Hebrew names for God used in that book and their meanings are listed, and throughout the New Testament we read the beautiful Name of **Yeshua**, Jesus.[3]

Here is an example of what reading the Psalms is like:

> O *Yahweh Elohim Tsebaoth*, who is like you?
> Mighty *Yah*, even your faithfulness surrounds you.
> —Psalm 89:8

Yahweh Tsebaoth, translated in English as Lord of Hosts, Lord Almighty, or Lord of Heaven's Armies, appears approximately 266 times in the Old Testament and twice (in Greek) in the New Testament.[4] This means that 268 times God chose to be described in the Bible in military terms.

I think this is part of the character of God with which we might initially feel uncomfortable. However, Yahweh Tsebaoth would not be the Lord of Heaven's Armies if it were not because of his perfect love, goodness, faithfulness, kindness, and justice. He is sovereign over all things and all that he is and does is perfect. Imagine it for a moment (and it's true, not just our imagination!)—God is a military commander who is slow to anger, never makes a mistake, is compassionate and merciful, and always acts justly.

> In your majesty ride forth victoriously in the cause of truth, humility and justice; let your right hand achieve awesome deeds.
> **PSALM 45:4**

---

3 The NOG version may be found on BibleGateway.com as hard copies are currently out of print.
4 The count varies a bit depending on the translation. See Romans 9:29 and James 5:4.

Further, as Webb and Oeste point out, God is "an uneasy war God who does not revel in battle or destruction and who grieves the mayhem that warfare inflicts on his creation."[5] His lament over the suffering of his people and even of their enemies is evidenced in passages such as Lamentations, Isaiah 15:5 and 16:11, and Jeremiah 48:35–36.

As we saw in Genesis in our brief glimpse into Eden and the subsequent fall of humans, God began his use of military force to rescue humanity. In fact, that bloody cross we talked about in the previous chapter—where soldiers hammered nails, and soldiers watched Jesus die, and soldiers declared the true identity of Christ—*that* cross was a military victory like none other. It was God's sacrificial love crushing Satan's head, followed by Christ's resurrection, which was a total trouncing of the enemy of death.[6]

OUR BATTLES AND GOD THE WARRIOR

We are all in battles throughout our life journeys. We are in battle against evil, within and without. We fight for our own flourishing and for the good of others. We wage war against discouragement, addictions, lies, and toxic relationships. We use the power of our words to try to persuade our children—and everyone else—to do the right thing, and with that same weapon we blast what we oppose. If God is the ultimate and perfect warrior, would we not want to connect with him as we fight our own battles?

> The tongue has the power of life and death.
> **PROVERBS 18:21a**

There have been times in my life when I have struggled to believe that I have the military backing of heaven looking out for me. Times when I've cried out to the Lord, "Do you see me? Why aren't you doing anything? Are you fighting for me? Are you fighting for my people? If you are fighting for us, why can't I see it or feel it?"

---

5 Webb and Oeste, *Bloody, Brutal, and Barbaric?* 290.
6 See Acts 2:23–24; Romans 6:9; 1 Corinthians 15:26, 35–58, 2 Timothy 1:9–10.

We're talking about battle here—we don't battle over things that don't matter. When we are in battle there is danger, smoke, damage, high stakes, and likely blood. I do not use this word lightly. I don't expect us to hear "God is a warrior" and then suddenly think everything is fine. It is not. Even in the unseen realm of the heavenlies, there is battle.[7]

Knowing God as Yahweh Tsebaoth does not make the very real battles of this life go away. What it does is make us realize we are *never alone* in any battle. Yahweh Tsebaoth, the Lord of Heaven's Armies, fights for us. He fights for us with love, because he is not only a warrior, but also a loving parent who carries us.

"Do not be terrified; do not be afraid of them. The Lord your God, who is going before you, **will fight for you**, as he did for you in Egypt, before your very eyes, and in the wilderness. There you saw how the Lord your God **carried you, as a father** carries his son, **all the way** you went until you reached this place" (Deuteronomy 1:29-31, emphasis mine).

Notice that this verse says God carries his people "all the way." Are some battles of this earth never ending until heaven? It seems that might be the case. If so, how do we keep going, even as we are often wounded and weary along the way?

Our military friends can help us here. They know dedicated service that often includes suffering. They persevere by keeping their ultimate goal in mind—whether it is the defense of their country, the protection of their loved ones, the guarding of freedom, or the defeat of an enemy who threatens the safety and well-being of a people group or nation. They know how to follow orders and support each other, and they continue doing that day after day, year after year.

Yahweh Tsebaoth is the perfect commander. He has given us marching orders for living our lives and fighting our battles. He is for the flourishing of humans. He is against injustice and evil.[8] He knows everything from the beginning to the end of all of life on this planet and into eternity. We must trust and follow him.

---

7 See Daniel 10.
8 See Deuteronomy 16:19-20; Isaiah 1:16-17, 58:6-7; Micah 6:8; Matthew 23:23; Hebrews 1:8-9; Revelation 11:15-19.

FIGHT OR BE STILL ... OR BOTH

There is another phenomenon that we should consider here. Sometimes God asks us to stop fighting and to be still because he is going to take care of matters, often in ways we could not pull off, however he chooses. Exodus 14:14 says, "The Lord will fight for you; you need only to be still." This was spoken by Moses to the people of Israel as they were being chased down by the powerful Egyptian army.

I have heard this "be still" phrase from the Lord repeatedly in the past few months. Loved ones of mine are in a rupturing relationship; people I care for deeply are choosing paths that hurt them and others. I often feel powerless to help. But as we will discuss later, there is fighting I can do on their behalf. I can love and I can pray. I can, as our friend Mike puts it, "hold space for hope."[9] But only Yahweh Tsebaoth is all-powerful, and he loves my people more than I do.

The military is not always engaged in combat. But they are trained and committed to being ready. For them to not take action and to be still is just as important at times as it is for them to become involved at other times. We need to continually pay attention to our Commander and follow his orders.

OUR RESPONSE TO YAHWEH TSEBAOTH

As we further consider our response to Yahweh Tsebaoth, let's learn again from a great military leader. In Joshua chapters 23 and 24 Joshua is now an old man. This passage recounts his final farewell to the people he led for many years.

Joshua reminds the Israelites throughout his farewell that God fought for them and gave them their victories.[10] The battles God fought alongside them and for them were to take territory God had commanded them to possess in order to bless those around them. God fought battles that were in line with his purposes for his people. He fought for them even as he called them to follow him, live for him, and be a witness to the world of him.

---

9 Mike Paterson uses this phrase, "holding space for hope" as a guide in his pastoral care ministry with Cadence International.
10 See Joshua 23:3, 5, 9–10 and Joshua 24:8, 10, 12–13.

The responses God wanted from his people as He fought for them are recorded here in Joshua 23–24:

- Be strong and courageous. Protect the territory you and God fought for.
- Be careful to obey God in everything. Do not be swayed by people around you who don't know or revere God.
- Be devoted to God alone; do not make allegiances with any kind of false god because false gods serve the enemy of your souls.
- Love the Lord your God. This warfare is about relationship as well as territory.
- Believe God's promises and respect his wrath.
- Serve God wholeheartedly from this day forward.
- Keep on, and keep on, choosing all of the above.

Yahweh is Israel's *Melek* and *Go'el*.
He is *Yahweh Tsebaoth*.
—Isaiah 44:6a (NOG)

Melek is Hebrew for King

Go'el is Hebrew for Redeemer, Defender

RECAP

The military provides us an earthly portrayal of a heavenly reality. God Himself is a warrior, and his angels are organized troops. Knowing Yahweh Tsebaoth, the Lord of Heaven's Armies, assures us and brings us very real help in our personal and relational battles. God is fighting for us with his actions of love. He asks us to trust him and follow his commands which are given for our flourishing.

SECTION 2

Callings

What does the Bible say to every Christian about our callings to be a spiritual soldier involved in spiritual warfare? Since spiritual pacifism is not an option for those who follow Jesus, we would be wise to prepare and engage.

CHAPTER 7

Christian Soldiers

IN 1865, A MINISTER and prolific author, Sabine Baring-Gould wrote words for children to sing as they walked from a place called Horbury Bridge to St. Peter's Church in Yorkshire. Originally titled "Hymn for Procession with Crosses and Banners," the lyrics together with a melody by Arthur Sullivan six years later became the well-known hymn, "Onward Christian Soldiers."[1]

> Onward Christian soldiers!
>   Marching as to war,
> With the cross of Jesus
>   going on before.
> Christ, the royal Master,
>   leads against the foe;
> Forward into battle,
>   see, His banners go!
>
> Onward, Christian soldiers!
>   Marching as to war,
> With the cross of Jesus,
>   Going on before.

---

[1] "Onward, Christian Soldiers," *Wikipedia*.

I find it interesting that these lyrics were first written for children. Baring-Gould himself says: "For a Whitsuntide [Pentecost] procession it was arranged that our school should join forces with that of a neighboring village. I wanted the children to sing when marching from one village to another, but couldn't think of anything quite suitable, so I sat up at night and resolved to write something myself. 'Onward, Christian Soldiers' was the result. It was written in great haste. . . . I am certain that nothing surprised me more than its popularity."[2]

The Apostle Paul, while writing to Timothy as a spiritual son, offered this strong admonishment: "Join with me in suffering, like a good soldier of Christ Jesus. No one serving as a soldier gets entangled in civilian affairs, but rather tries to please his commanding officer" (2 Timothy 2:3-4).

Here is a truth for every one of us right now. Paul's words were not only for Timothy in the first century, and Sabine's hymn lyrics were not limited to children in 1865. Every person, no matter how young or old, who confesses Jesus as Savior and Lord is a spiritual soldier. For each and every Christian, the "march and music of military in the Bible" is personal. It is global. It is practical. It is essential.

EZER

In Genesis 1:26-28 and 2:18-24, I believe God gives humans an underlying modus operandi, or method of operation, for how he intends for them carry out the grand mandate, his creation commission. God calls them to rule and care for the earth (leadership and stewardship), be fruitful and multiply (relationship and impact), be his image, and to march forward into the battle of good and evil begun in Genesis 3. In her book, *Being God's Image*, Dr. Imes says that when God makes humans in his image, it is more than bearing his image, it is *being* his image. "Being God's image involves both kinship and kingship."[3] Note that this commission is not about whether one is married or not, or has children. These callings from God are embedded in each of us—in our humanity.

---

2 "Onward, Christian Soldiers | Hymnary.Org.
3 Imes, *Being God's Image: Why Creation Still Matters*, 32.

God breathed the breath of eternal life into the first person he lovingly made from the dust of the earth. He immediately set humans apart from the rest of the creation by giving the first "adam" (Hebrew for human) responsibility over other living creatures. Then God said: "It is not good for man to be alone" (Genesis 2:18). I do not believe God was talking about loneliness here. The context is proxy leadership given by God to the humans he was creating (and all humans to follow). God's completion of his leadership mantle over the earth was to provide an "ezer kenegdo" to Adam. "Ezer" is the Hebrew word for strong, powerful, military help. It is also a word for rescue—as in life saving. And the ezer in Genesis 2 is described as "corresponding to"—like the right hand is to the left hand— "kenegdo."[4]

The word ezer (the initial "e" is pronounced like a long "a") is used as a noun 21 times in the Old Testament, twice for woman, three times for military aid, and 16 times for God providing warrior-like help to his people.[5] Here is one example from Deuteronomy 33:29.

> Blessed are you, Israel!
>   Who is like you,
>   a people saved by the Lord?
> He is your shield and helper [ezer]
>   and your glorious sword.
> Your enemies will cower before you,
>   and you will tread on their heights.

Ezer has a military connotation, and ezer is what God calls the person he is making from Adam's side to serve with him in carrying out the Commander's orders to lead, steward, co-create, image him to the world, and battle for good. This ezer is a woman. She is kenegdo—corresponding to—neither his inferior nor superior, as we see in Genesis 2:21–24 ("bone of my bone and flesh of my flesh"). Dr. Imes writes "Ezer is primarily used in military contexts and is best translated 'ally.'"[6] The fact that the woman's warrior help directly corresponds to the man infers that he is also a warrior.

---

4 Carolyn Custis James, *Lost Women of the Bible*, chapter 1.
5 For examples, see Exodus 18:4; Deuteronomy 33:7 and 26; Psalm 20:2, 33:20, and 121:1–2.
6 Imes, *Being God's Image: Why Creation Still Matters*, 40.

We could observe the scarcity of female examples of career military women in the Bible and wonder how this connects to ezer. What if we looked at every woman in the Bible as one within whom the spirit of "warrior" is embedded, and for that matter, every man as well? What ways, other than combat, did women fight in the Scripture? Consider the Hebrew midwives in Exodus 1, Ruth and Naomi in the book of Ruth, Mary Magdalene in the Gospels, and Priscilla in the book of Acts. How did they as ezers battle?

Why such strong language to describe God's intentions for his humans on planet Earth? I believe it is because it will take *that kind of military strength* to carry out God's purposes—purposes that he did not ask them to pursue without *his* ezer-strong warrior help.

What is the underlying modus operandi which the Creator intended in Genesis 2:18–24? It is **together**—male and female.[7] And **with help**—with the help of each other, with God's help, and even with the help of the heavenly hosts. This is how we fulfill our commission.

Our friend Ryan Padgett, now retired from the military, described his basic training as a time when "we couldn't even go to the latrine without our battle buddy." If someone was found alone, the first question asked was, "Where is your battle buddy?" Ryan wisely noted, "If your battle buddy had a shortcoming, you would help them out—then you would both succeed. We were trained in this mentality. I wish we could have this as Christians." He went on to say that in a foxhole you shared the same air, were in the same danger, covered with the same grime, and had the same mission as your battle buddy. Foxholes were placed in proximity of others so that you not only literally had each other's back, but you could see and cover vulnerable areas of your people in other foxholes, forming a line of protection. He added, "In life, my wife shares the same foxhole with me."[8]

BATTLE

In the Old Testament, the word "battle" appears 207 times. War or warrior is noted about 287 times (NIV). Conflict is prevalent throughout Scripture.

---

7   We could add combinations also shown in Scripture like young and old, Jew and Gentile.
8   Conversation in 2023 with Ryan V. Padgett, TSgt, USAF (Ret.), Loadmaster, C-5M Super Galaxy.

Many of these references are about specific battles, but some have to do with the overall battle of good and evil, life and death, God's kingdom and the dominion of darkness.[9]

It is in this overall battle that every Christian is called to participate—together, with help. Yahweh Tsebaoth is the King. The kingdom of God is the territory we are fighting for.[10] Christian soldiers come from every nation of the world.[11] Our citizenship is in heaven.[12] Our enemy is not a human one but evil fallen angelic beings, the devil and his minions.[13] The battle will continue throughout our lives until the Day of God's Judgment.[14]

In the next chapter we will look specifically at God's instructions and provisions for us in this battle. For now, let us take a look at verses three and four of Baring-Gould's hymn. Here we see the themes of "together with help," unity (not to be confused with uniformity), the legacy of faithful Christian soldiers before us, and the certainty of victory in Christ.

GOD'S CREATION COMMISSION FOR HUMANS IS ABOUT:
Leadership
Stewardship
Relationship
Impact
Image
Battle

> Like a mighty army
>   moves the church of God.
> Brothers, we are treading
>   where the saints have trod.
> We are not divided;
>   all one body we,
> One in hope and doctrine,
>   one in charity.

---

9 See Ephesians 2:1–2 and Colossians 1:13.
10 See John 3:1–21, Revelation 12:10.
11 See Revelation 5:9–10, 7:9, 14:6–7.
12 See Ephesians 2:19, Philippians 3:20.
13 See 1 Peter 5:8–9.
14 See John 12:31–32, 2 Corinthians 5:9–10, Jude 6, Revelation 20.

Crowns and thrones may perish,
    kingdoms rise and wane,
But the church of Jesus
    constant will remain.
Gates of hell can never
    'gainst that church prevail;
We have Christ's own promise,
    and that cannot fail

Onward, Christian soldiers!
    Marching as to war,
With the cross of Jesus,
    Going on before.[15]

Do you hear God calling you to be a spiritual warrior? Do you understand that he made you a warrior because he knew this is what it would take to follow him on this earth? Are you all in? Then let's get more specific about this calling.

---

15 "Onward Christian Soldiers," public domain.

CHAPTER 8

Stand Your Ground

I RECENTLY HAD the honor of talking with a couple of Sailors who that day had successfully completed their Navy SEAL BUD/S training.[1] They were not only exhausted, but so excited about this accomplishment and looked forward to the rigor that was still to come. They volunteered for this challenge and they were giving it their all. Some of their friends had also given it their all and unfortunately had to "ring the bell" because of serious enough challenges forcing them to stop training and leave the SEAL program.

Maybe you did not realize that you became a spiritual military person when you put your faith in Jesus. Or perhaps you think that if your spiritual fervor is not at "SEAL level" you are not needed. Realistically, most of us aren't equipped to be Special Forces. But every person's place in the mission of advancing and defending God's kingdom and gospel is vital. Not one of us can be idle or careless in these matters without it affecting the whole of the people of God and the mission of God.

Every believer in Christ is called to spiritual warfare. What spiritual battle might look like for you could be very different than for another Christian. In this calling we are not left without clear instructions and resources. We are given the Word of God, the people of God, the Spirit of God, and the

---

[1] SEAL is Sea, Air, and Land Teams. BUD/S training is Basic Underwater Demolition/SEAL.

armor of God to carry out the mission of God—which is always about his love moving toward humanity in rescue, redemption, and restoration.

Each of us has been given ground, or territory, that is ours to steward, lead, and protect. Whether it is our bodies, homes, families, jobs, callings, giftings, relationships, positions, or responsibilities—we have been given ground. Ephesians 6:13 says, "Stand your ground . . . and after you have done everything . . . stand!"

THE ARMOR OF GOD

Ephesians 6:10–18 is a power-packed passage. Here the Apostle Paul details the armor of God, which is needed by, and available to, every believer. My husband David and I have taught and preached together through a ten-week course we developed on these verses. Someday I hope to write it all out in a book of its own. For now, let me share with you a brief overview of our study.

Finally, be strong in the Lord and in his mighty power (v. 10)

This is not a suggestion, it is a command; therefore, we can assume it is doable. It hearkens to the marching orders given directly from the Lord to Joshua at the beginning of his military book.[2] The strength we need is not our own, it is the Lord's, and we are connected to Him—this is the "together" that establishes our battle stance.

We have other allies in the battle as well. I like to think of them as A–B–C: Angels, Believers, and Christ himself. Angels are portrayed in Scripture as warriors who fight on our behalf.[3] As Jesus prayed for his followers before he went to the cross, he focused on unity as one of the ways his people would be protected from the evil one.[4] Christian brothers and sisters need each other; we were made to battle together as allies.[5] And Christ himself is with us, for us, in us, and working towards our victory and our good.[6]

---

2 See Joshua 1:6–9.
3 See Daniel 10; Hebrew 1:7, 14; Revelation 12:7–8.
4 See John 17:11–19.
5 See 1 Peter 5:8–9.
6 See Romans 8:26–39.

***Put on the full armor of God so that you can take your stand against the devil's schemes* (v. 11)**
The devil is our enemy. I cannot say it strongly enough. Please listen here: the devil is not our friend—never was, never will be. He does not have one teeny tiny nice or sort-of-nice thought about any of us. His intentions toward us are *always* to "steal, kill, and destroy" (John 10:10a). It is complete nonsense for us to make the smallest agreement or alliance with this enemy. We must stand against him in every way every day. Because this is war!

The devil is a schemer and constantly working against humans. He has been refining and practicing his wicked strategies for thousands of years. But here is the good news: We are not unaware of his schemes.[7] We have been told what they are in the Bible. We can see how he has operated through history. In fact, each piece of the full armor that God gives us directly corresponds to, combats, and protects us against a scheme or tactic of the enemy.

***For our struggle is not against flesh and blood, but against the rulers, against the authorities, against the powers of this dark world and against the spiritual forces of evil in the heavenly realms* (v. 12)**
Sometimes we get confused about where these enemies fall in the order of spiritual power. Let's clarify right now: Jesus and Satan are not even remotely on the same level. Jesus is God. Satan is a fallen angel. Humans are not angels, and they do not become angels when they go to heaven. Angels stay as angels in eternity and humans remain humans through eternity. Angels have a different level of spiritual power than do humans, yet in heaven humans will judge the angels.[8] Angels and demons (fallen angels) are not everywhere at the same time—but God is! They are not all-powerful—but God is! And they do not know everything—but God does!

We also sometimes get confused about where our spiritual battle energy is to be spent. This verse clearly tells us it is not people who are our enemies, but evil spiritual forces. This sounds scary, and that is why verse 10 comes first. Our strength is in the Lord who is greater than any enemy, seen or unseen.[9]

---

7 See 2 Corinthians 2:11.
8 See Psalm 103:20–21, 2 Peter 2:11, 1 Corinthians 6:3.
9 See 1 John 4:4.

Therefore, put on the full armor of God, so that when the day of evil comes you may be able to stand your ground, and after you have done everything, to stand (v. 13)
Note the choice we are given here. The armor of God is available and effective, but we get to choose whether we put it on. Remember from chapter one that God respects us enough to honor our volition.

Also note that it is not *if* but *when* the day of evil comes. Yet there is a confidence here—we are told to do everything we can, and then to stand. Yes, spiritual warfare will involve fighting, but even more, it will involve standing—not giving any ground to the enemy who hates us. This is our kingdom territory that we are called to defend. We are in a battle that has already been decided by the King of kings and Lord of lords as his victory. So, while we take the enemy and his attacks seriously, we also don't panic.[10] We stand.

Stand firm then, with the belt of truth buckled around your waist (v. 14a)
The devil is a liar; lying is his native language and scheme. "He is a liar and the father of lies" (John 8:44b). But our center of gravity is covered with the belt of truth—God's truth. We recognize and refute lies. We make decisions based on God's wisdom. When we hear whispers such as, "You are a washout, you can never be forgiven of this one, you are not needed, you are unlovable," we must fight to not let any of those lies occupy real estate in our minds and hearts.

As Paul puts it in 2 Corinthians 10:3-5 "For though we live in the world, we do not wage war as the world does. The weapons we fight with are not the weapons of the world. On the contrary, they have divine power to demolish strongholds. We demolish arguments and every pretension that sets itself up against the knowledge of God, and we take captive every thought to make it obedient to Christ."

With the breastplate of righteousness in place (v. 14b)
In Ephesians 6 Paul is picturing armor that a Roman soldier wore in the

---

10 Note, I understand that the devil is not our only enemy; the world's system and our old self—"Sarx"—are also our enemies. I am not focusing on them in this study. See 1 John 2:15-17, Romans 7:5-6, 8:4-13, and Galatians 5:16-24.

first century. Perhaps military people whom we have already met in this book, like Cornelius, sometimes wore this uniform to work. The breastplate covered one's vital organs—the heart, liver, kidneys, stomach, and lungs. It was good protection against an enemy's sword or arrow.

Our enemy is called "the accuser." The Bible says the devil accuses Christians night and day.[11] He is relentless in his attempt to smear believers with shame. Remember, he is a liar, so right away you know his accusations are not true. As a child of God you are literally covered with a righteousness that is perfect, eternal, and un-tarnishable. It is the righteousness of Christ![12] "Therefore, there is now no condemnation for those who are in Christ Jesus" (Romans 8:1).

But there is more. We are also called to live righteously—to choose right over wrong, light over darkness, love over fear, obedience to God over self-centeredness. And this righteous living is also a protection. It is a beacon of light and a blessing to the world.[13]

The protection of the breastplate of righteousness is lived out like this: "When the devil comes knocking on your door simply say, 'Jesus, it's for you.'"[14]

> The difference between the voice of the Accuser and the voice of the Holy Spirit is that the Accuser attacks our identity with derogatory labels, and the Holy Spirit confirms our identity as beloved, then gently and specifically corrects our behavior.

***And with your feet fitted with the readiness that comes from the gospel of peace* (v. 15)**
The devil is a thief—a criminal who ruthlessly aims to rob us of life, joy, peace, purpose, and all good things. And how does he attempt to take our ground? A little at a time.

---

11 See Revelation 12:10.
12 See Romans 3:21–24.
13 See Psalm 23:3, 37:6, 103:17.
14 Robin Jones Gunn, *Sunsets*, 179.

THE WORD ON THE WORD:
WHAT THE BIBLE SAYS ABOUT ITSELF
by David Schroeder

God's Word is *alive*,
active, sharper than a sword.
It penetrates to soul and spirit,
joints and marrow, and it judges the
thoughts and attitudes
of the heart. It is God-breathed,
divine revelation,
inspired, prophetic, poetic, and powerful.
It is perfect, true, flawless, pure,
sure, right, radiant, gold,
trustworthy, reliable,
deep, rich, consecrated, and *unchained*.

God's Word is a seed imperishable,
a rock immovable,
a force unstoppable, a power unimaginable, a truth irrefutable,
a love undeniable,
a treasure unsurpassed, and a knowledge unequaled.
It should dwell in us richly, abide in us deeply,
transform us completely,
anchor us firmly, and mobilize us boldly.

©David Schroeder 2016

It is useful for *teaching*, rebuking, correcting,
guiding, training, claiming, proclaiming, preaching,
encouraging, comforting,
illuminating, convicting, celebrating, mobilizing, stirring,
challenging, galvanizing, spreading,
growing, sustaining,
healing, calibrating, and *giving hope*.

It is our promised inheritance.
It is the *Word of life*,
the Word of grace, and the Word of the Lord.
The person who follows God's Word will be
wise, blessed, godly,
righteous, holy, pardoned, redeemed, sanctified,
delighted, joy-filled, rewarded,
fruitful, fed, full, and satisfied.

Above all, it is an amazing love letter
from the heart of God to His *beloved* children and
IT WILL REMAIN FOREVER!

In complete contrast, Jesus proclaimed His purpose: "I have come that they may have life, and have it abundantly" (John 10:10). This is good news, also known as the gospel. "Christ has died, Christ is risen, Christ will come again" is often quoted on Sundays, but it is truth for every day. It is because of the death, resurrection, and certainty of Christ's return that we can walk through the battles of this world with settled peace.

We are ready to stand our ground against the enemy's scheme to steal, kill, and destroy when we have gospel feet, walking securely in the truth that nothing can separate us from the love of Christ as we share this good news with others.[15]

In addition to all this, take up the shield of faith with which you can extinguish all the flaming arrows of the evil one (v. 16)

The Apostle Peter tells us in 1 Peter 5:8 that the devil is a predator—a roaring lion seeking whom he may devour. Let us not miss the fact that he is roaring, thus often giving away his location. Still, we must be on the alert. We need to resist him, as Peter goes on to say in verse 9, "standing firm in the faith." Do you see that word again—stand?

Take up the shield of faith. It's not flippant or flimsy; it's substantial and heavy. Like a Roman shield, it is covered with leather and dipped in water. Can you hear the sound when arrows on fire hit it? *Sizzle, sizzle.*

Faith is belief in action. We can talk all we want about what we believe, but if the way we live does not align with our words we are vulnerable to the enemy's flaming arrows and sharp teeth. Hebrews 11 shows us that a life of walking in true faith is possible and has been accomplished by many ordinary and extraordinary people who have gone before us.

Take the helmet of salvation (v. 17a)

The enemy is a seducer, masquerading as an angel of light.[16] He is bent on deception. He takes truths and twists them. He abuses desires and pawns them. He makes counterfeits and tantalizes with them. He treats us as fools who don't know any better.

---

15 See Romans 8:37–39.
16 See 2 Corinthians 11:14.

Ah, but that is where the devil is wrong. We are not that easily fooled. Because we have put on the helmet of salvation, our thoughts are controlled by who we truly are in Christ, and our identities are secure in him. We are children of the light and of day, we are aware of the enemy's seductions, and we remain "clearheaded" (1 Thessalonians 5:4–11 NLT).

And the sword of the Spirit, which is the word of God (v. 17b)

The enemy is a tempter, harassing all people throughout history, and even using his best enticing skills on Jesus. But Jesus was not derailed by the tailor-made-for-him temptations.[17] And we don't need to be either. We have the sword of the Spirit, which is the Bible, also known as the Word of God. There is no book, resource, weapon, or soul-food like the Bible. Read again how my husband, David, beautifully describes this Word on the previous pages.

This is what Jesus used to combat the temptations He faced. It is a sharp two-edged sword. It can do damage to the enemy, and it can keep us on the side of battle that knows and does what is good and right.[18]

And pray in the Spirit on all occasions with all kinds of prayers and requests. With this in mind, be alert, and always keep on praying for all the saints. (v. 18)

Finally, the devil is the evil one.[19] He is not to be messed with, given in to, or followed in any way. Over all our battle strategies against the schemes of the enemy, our covering is to be prayer. Prayer involves both talking and listening to God.

Warfare prayer is to pray about anything and everything—anytime, anywhere, always. This prayer is "in the Spirit" which I like to think of as making the armor of God (including that heavy shield) feel like workout activewear. We can move about with confidence and freedom because we know we have access to the throne room of the God of the universe 24/7.[20]

---

17 See 1 Thessalonians 3:5, Matthew 4:2–11.
18 See Hebrews 4:12, Luke 10:16–20, and Psalm 119: 9, 105.
19 See John 17:15.
20 See Hebrews 4:16.

"So when I fight, I'll fight on my knees, with my hands lifted high. Oh God, the battle belongs to You!"[21] This powerful song by Phil Wickham says it well.

Let us not miss Paul's call to pray for all Christ-followers (saints). Spiritual battle should not and cannot be successfully carried out alone. Who are your battle buddies? Just as Roman soldiers fought in lines and regularly employed the testudo, or tortoise formation (shield wall), we too must work with, and on behalf of, each other. No Christian is exempt from following Ephesians 6.

Remember, your spot in the kingdom of God is important. Your work in the mission of God is vital. And your ground is just that—**yours**. Defend and steward it well.

---

21 *Battle Belongs,* by songwriters Brian Johnson and Philip David Wickham.

CHAPTER 9

Reveille, Retreat, and Taps

TWO TIMES A day at every military installation of the United States, people walking or driving in cars come to a complete stop. The exact timing of these stops varies by installation, but the protocol remains the same. When Reveille Morning Colors plays in the morning or Retreat Evening Colors plays at sunset, all military personnel in uniform stop wherever they are, stand at attention, and face the flag which is raised at Reveille and lowered at Retreat. When "To the Colors" begins playing, they salute. Those not in uniform and civilians must stop, be quiet, and pull to the side of the road if driving. When Taps signals the end of day at 9 or 10 p.m., it is time for all to pause (not necessarily pull over to the side of the road) to remember those who gave their lives in service for their country. It is also a signal for rest in preparation to continue the mission tomorrow.

These practices and protocols are long established. But this is more than routine ritual to military people; it is about respect. It is about pausing to honor what is important, to recalibrate perspective, and to unify purpose.

All of us who are Christian soldiers need this kind of rhythm in our daily lives. We need the daily pauses, the faithful practices, and recalibrated perspectives.

It seems God has his own Reveille and Retreat. Look at Psalm 65:8:

> The whole earth is filled with awe at your wonders;
> where morning dawns, where evening fades,
> you call forth songs of joy.

The warrior, David, had a protocol of prayer to start and end his day.

> In the morning, Lord, you hear my voice;
> in the morning I lay my requests before you
> and wait expectantly.
> —Psalm 5:3

> But I will sing of your strength,
> in the morning I will sing of your love;
> for you are my fortress,
> my refuge in times of trouble.
> —Psalm 59:16

> May my prayer be set before you like incense;
> may the lifting up of my hands be like the evening sacrifice.
> —Psalm 141:2

INDIVIDUAL SPIRITUAL RHYTHMS

What are your personal spiritual rhythms? Some of mine are regular Bible reading and study, prayer throughout the day, weekly church attendance and involvement, ministry using my unique giftings, reading and listening to wise people, and spiritual conversation with friends who are also seeking to deeply know and wholeheartedly follow God.

These spiritual behaviors do not make me a Christian any more than saluting a flag makes someone a military person. Jesus made me a Christian when I as a child put my faith in him. "In Christ alone my hope is found."[1]

---

[1] This is one of my all-time favorite songs, *In Christ Alone*, by Stuart Townend & Keith Getty Copyright © 2001 Thankyou Music.

These practices are for my health and maturity as well as for equipping me to do my part in the kingdom work that has my name on it.[2]

Maybe reading and studying the Bible is new to you. Maybe the Bible has been part of your life for many years. The Bible is a shining light, living and active, a sharp sword, God-breathed, holy, and eternal.[3] I've written an appendix to this book that might also be helpful in your understanding and appreciation of the Bible.[4]

I find it fitting that the Bible is described as food.[5] Food is something every human needs every day, no matter how much food they ate when they were a child, or last year, or when they were especially hungry. You see where I'm going with this. Food is essential; God's Word is essential. Furthermore, all food does not taste the same. The food of Scripture contains all kinds of holistic nutrition. Some days you might be reading and it "tastes" as bland as plain oatmeal. And some days Bible study is like a gourmet feast. It's okay if you do not feel very inspired while reading a certain chapter or book. Read it anyway. Your soul needs its nourishment. Oatmeal is good for you (and to some of us it tastes good too).

We talked earlier about prayer involving communicating with God about anything anytime anywhere always. The practice of praying before meals is a helpful rhythmic pause, which seemed to also be the pattern of Jesus and his followers.[6] Prayer before meals is a great way for us to practice gratitude several times a day.

I encourage you to also teach your children to pray before consuming meals. A memorized prayer or song for young ones is lovely. When I was growing up, our family often recited together: "Before we eat this food, dear Lord, we bow our heads to pray. And for Thy love and all Thy gifts, our grateful thanks we say. In Jesus' name, Amen." Some of our grandkids sing to the tune of Frère Jacques: "Thank you Jesus, Thank you Jesus, for our food, for our food. Thank You for our mommy, thank You for our daddy, thank You for our teacher, thank You for (and the list goes on . . .), Amen, Amen."

---

2 See Ephesians 2:10.
3 See Psalm 119:130, 160; Hebrews 4:12; 2 Timothy 3:16; 1 Peter 1:23; 2 Peter 2:1-2.
4 See Appendix A.
5 See Joshua 1:8, Isaiah 59:21, Jeremiah 15:16, Amos 8:11, 1 Peter 2:1-3.
6 See Matthew 14:19, 15:36, 26:26-27; Mark 6:41, 8:6-7, 14:23; Luke 9:16-19, 24:30; John 6:11; Acts 27:35.

I have heard on occasion that we should show reverence to God by not asking him for petty requests, as though somehow he is not to be bothered by our everyday human concerns. I disagree. My Lord says he counts the hairs on my head.[7] This is attention to detail! And let's add, when I brush my hair, he re-counts. The Mighty God of the Universe knows every cell in our bodies and he cares more than we have a clue about. Let us bring him all our thoughts and prayers, whether big or small, spoken or unspoken.

I don't know where I first learned the prayer acronym A.C.T.S.—Adoration, Confession, Thanksgiving, and Supplication (which is a big word for "ask"). While there have been only a few seasons in my life when I have regularly written out prayers in each category, it has served to help me remember to include praise, repentance, and worship along with my requests.

Then there is listening. God speaks to us through his Word, his creation, his people, his Spirit (promptings, reminders, gut checks, conviction of sin, clearer understanding, healing, etc.), and his circumstances (that are never random). He also speaks to us with his voice, which isn't necessarily a "different" voice than ours in our head when we walk with God.[8] Often we forget to take a moment to listen to the next thoughts that come to mind after we have asked God what he wants us to know or do. Sometimes those very words are the beginning of our answers. We need to regularly pause to listen, pay attention, and seek God's heart. We have the wonderful promise that when we seek him, we will find him.[9]

TOGETHER SPIRITUAL RHYTHMS

Perhaps you have heard people say, "I don't go to church because the church is full of hypocrites." And they are not wrong. However, I wonder, would we rather that church was some elite group of do-gooders within which we likely wouldn't feel like we belong? Have we read the stories of real people in the real Bible who had real interesting and sometimes real awful, painful, hypocritical, or confusing lives?

---

7 See Matthew 10:30, Luke 12:7.
8 See Romans 5:5, 1 Corinthians 2:6, Philippians 4:6–7.
9 See Deuteronomy 4:29, Jeremiah 29:13, Luke 11:9–10, Acts 17:26–27.

Church is made up of real people. You will meet trustworthy God-seeking real-deal people of faith. And you will meet some people there whose words don't match up with their actions. There will be those who know a lot about God and those who know little. But church is not a competition. It is a fellowship to which we are called. It is a place and a people who pause to listen, learn, love, and live out their faith. I highly recommend a healthy church as part of a healthy spiritual rhythm.

Let's talk for a minute about our friends. If you are a Christian, I hope not all your friends are Christians. I hope you have good relationships with great people who don't believe like you do. You need them and they need you.

If you are reading this and do not yet believe in Jesus, I ask you to not write him off. Please consider not permitting the pain humans have caused you to keep you from the God who loves you perfectly. I hope you won't let legitimate questions and doubts keep you away from the One who knows everything (and does not expect you to know or understand everything). Can you look only at Jesus right now? Who is he? Could you give him a chance?

If you are a Christian and you do not have real-deal Christian friends in your life these days, let's stop right now and ask God for them. You need them and they need you. We all need friends who will see us, tell us the truth, point us to Jesus, and help us fight the good fight.

My long-time friend Jerri will sometimes listen to me talk for a little while and then reply with the word "nonsense." It might sound like she is being a mean friend to me, but she's actually being kind. "Nonsense" is a word we use in our friendship to signal each other when we realize that the other's thought patterns are going down a harmful path. When we are believing lies of the enemy or buying into false narratives and cannot see clearly, we say to each other, "That sounds like nonsense." It helps to snap us out of that negative cycle and redirect the conversation to more productive paths. I hope you have, or will have, at least one friend in your life who will be able to tell you when you are in the realm of nonsense.

Military people know and live the value of "together." The U.S. Army creed includes, "I am a Warrior and a member of a team." The U.S. Airman creed says, "I will never leave an Airman behind." The Marine Corps motto: "Semper Fi," means always faithful and loyal. And Navy

Sailors serve with Honor, Courage, and Commitment—"to work together as a team."[10]

Jesus said this, "A new command I give you: Love one another. As I have loved you, so you must love one another. By this everyone will know that you are my disciples, if you love one another" (John 13:34–35).

The writer of Hebrews put it this way: "Let us hold unswervingly to the hope we profess, for he who promised is faithful. And let us consider how we may spur one another on toward love and good deeds, not giving up meeting together, as some are in the habit of doing, but encouraging one another—and all the more as you see the Day approaching" (Hebrews 10:23–25).

TAPS

Twenty-four notes make up a tune that stirs the heart like few other short melodies do. Perhaps the 35 notes of Amazing Grace have a similar effect. But in the 24 notes of Taps there is grief, longing, and pondering. Pause for a few seconds and hear the song in your mind if you know it. If you are not familiar with it, listen online to a bugler play this song and pay attention to your own reaction.[11]

Taps reminds us of the truth of Ecclesiastes 7:2.

> It is better to go to a house of mourning
>   than to go to a house of feasting,
> for death is the destiny of everyone;
>   the living should take this to heart.

This verse is real in my life. In the summer of 2021, I along with my brothers and my mom, family and friends, stood by my father's grave. Part of what we shared at that graveside was this verse from Ecclesiastes; it was one my dad often spoke about at funerals.

What could be good about mourning? Mourning helps us feel the depths of our humanity which is mortal. And in that mortality, we are joined by Jesus, who chose to take on a human body and go all the way

---

10 "United States Navy > About > Our Core Values."
11 "WELCOME TO TAPS BUGLER," tapsbugler.com.

to the grave with that body. Mourning also takes us beyond this earth and certain death to what is promised us because Jesus came back to life and conquered death—eternal life. Standing by our dad's grave I grieved, but not as one without hope.[12] Mourning helps us take a good look at our lives in light of eternity.

Taps is an invitation to recalibrate perspective. Author Randy Alcorn says, "The Bible tells us that while men may not remember or care what our lives here have been, God remembers perfectly and cares very much—so much that the door of eternity swings on the hinges of choices made here and now."[13]

Alcorn goes on to say, "Your life on earth is a dot. From that dot extends a line that goes on for all eternity. Right now you're living *in* the dot. But what are you living *for*? Are you living for the dot or for the line? Are you living for earth or for heaven? Are you living for the short today or the long tomorrow?"[14]

I can tell you with great joy that my father knew and lived for Jesus. He was very intentional about his earthly choices in light of eternity. The man I knew as my dad at home was consistent with the man who preached around the world and was a leader in a missionary organization focused on the military. His life impacted countless people as he and Mom shared the gospel, shared their lives, and helped people know and walk with God. I'd love for you to experience his story. It is online at Cadence.org/DickPattyMemorial.

In the autumn of final edits on this book in 2024, my mom also relocated to heaven. Vibrant and active at age 96, she was driving herself to the store one week, then in the hospital with stage four cancer the next week, and on to Glory eight days later. As I said at her memorial service, "It happened fast. But we felt the timing, the presence, and the provision of God every step of this journey. We are so proud of how our mom lived and how she died." Hers was a beautiful testimony of generous love and steadfast faith. I invite you to experience the blessing of this saint at Cadence.org/MargaretPattyMemorial.

---

12 See 1 Thessalonians 4:13–14.
13 Randy Alcorn, *In Light of Eternity*, p. 141.
14 Alcorn, p 143.

Dear Reader, your life is a gift. It is a treasure. You were carefully created by a wise God who never makes mistakes.[15] You have people to love, work to accomplish, and a God you can know. In ways we do understand and in ways we do not understand, our lives matter. They matter not only during our time on the planet, but for eternity. What will you do with your "dot"—your one precious life?

> Day is done, Gone the sun,
> From the lake, From the hill,
> From the sky.
> All is well, Safely rest,
> God is nigh.
> **LYRICS TO TAPS**

---

15 See Psalm 139.

SECTION 3

Courage

We all need more courage, don't we? What we have talked about so far is not light nor easy. This section isn't either. But maybe it will help us with perspective, with pacing, and with perseverance. Three themes are presented in these chapters: the kingdom of God, the music of the love of Jesus, and clarification of our marching orders between now and eternity.

CHAPTER 10

Conquering King

LET US LOOK at the kingdom to which Christians belong. This is our "true country," where our allegiance is centered and for whose causes we fight.

KINGDOM OF GOD

The words king and kingdom show up more than 2,500 times in the Bible, with 263 of those located in the New Testament and primarily related to Jesus Christ and his kingdom. In many ways the military and kingdoms or countries are linked together. A military or security force is tasked with protecting a country's or kingdom's constitution and constituency.

As Christians we are connected to a kingdom that is not of this world, and our responsibility as spiritual soldiers goes beyond earthly borders, patriotism, and people groups. I believe if we continue to learn the history of this kingdom, get to know the King of this kingdom, and understand the purposes of the kingdom of God, we will be able to better represent and defend this kingdom.

It is important for us to see that God's kingdom Story, carried throughout the Old Testament and New Testament included all nations.[1] Furthermore, the stunning description of the New Jerusalem in Revelation 21:23–26 tells

---

1 See Genesis 22:17–18, 26; 1 Chronicles 16:24; 2 Chronicles 20:6; Psalm 22:27, 67:1–2, 86:9; Isaiah 2:2, 52:10, 56:7; Haggai 2:7.

us that all the nations of the world—past, present, and future—will add their specific glory to the glory that is heaven.

> The city does not need the sun or the moon to shine on it, for the glory of God gives it light, and the Lamb is its lamp. The nations will walk by its light, and the kings of the earth will bring their splendor into it. On no day will its gates ever be shut, for there will be no night there. The glory and honor of the nations will be brought into it.

KING AND MESSIAH

Let's go back to the soundtrack of Genesis, the delightful melody of a good creation turned dissonant by the disobedience of humans and the resulting banishment from Eden. The curse upon the enemy and upon the ground resulted in hardship and suffering in the "earth-tasks" given by God to man and woman together. Redemption plays its own song all the way through—through what the enemy meant for evil but God turned to good in the selling of Joseph by his brothers and the resulting shackles of Egypt. Through the exodus on dry land in the midst of the Red Sea, and through the wilderness; through the conquests of Joshua; through the times of judges, prophets, and kings; through the fall and rebuilding of the country of Israel and the city of Jerusalem; through 400 years of "silence" with no new revelation from God—through all these years and events, Redemption's song was always part of the music.[2]

And then . . .

Remember that military angel choir who gave what I imagine was the greatest gospel-style anthem the world has ever heard:

> Glory to God in the highest heaven,
> and on earth peace to those on whom his favor rests.[3]

---

2 See Genesis 37, 39–47, then Genesis 50:20; Exodus 12–17; Deuteronomy 8; Joshua–2 Chronicles; Ezra–Nehemiah.
3 Luke 2:14.

King Jesus, both man and Messiah-God, was born. God of eternity stepped into time. God of the universe came to live on the planet Earth. God of creation took the form of a human creature. God of perfection made his home under the curse.

This Jesus, who is indeed the King of kings and Lord of lords, did not use his military might in the way people expected. Instead of overpowering, he came with mercy. Instead of punishment, he came with grace. Instead of judgment, he came with forgiveness. And instead of condemnation, he came with love.

But let us not fool ourselves; Messiah Jesus was no enabling weakling. He did not wink at sin nor sanction any abuse. He was protective of the poor and powerless. He had very harsh words for arrogant and oppressive religious leaders. He did *not* play favorites, and he *did* undermine unjust systems of the day, such as slavery and patriarchy. As MA (Theology) student and Royal Canadian Air Force Captain (Retired) Jazmine Lawrence put it, "Jesus countered temptation with Scripture, sickness with healing, and social hierarchies with love."[4] He was a conquering king like no other.

The cross of Jesus was a permanent military victory. In choosing to die in this way, Jesus took on himself the punishment for every wrong thought, action, and reaction of every human who ever lived or will live. He became cursed for us to save us. "Christ has rescued us from the curse . . . he took upon himself the curse for our wrongdoing" (Galatians 3:13 NLT). His innocence made our justification possible. His honor covered our shame. Jesus' death destroyed death.[5] His resurrection took down the enemy's biggest weapon against us. And if we have personally responded to Jesus with belief, we are redeemed; we are free! The battle for our souls has been won. Let's celebrate this amazing grace: "Therefore, there is no condemnation for those who are in Christ Jesus" (Romans 8:1).

HIS KINGDOM COME

Jesus described his kingdom to us in ways we could not predict. He said it was for those who were poor in spirit, persecuted for righteousness, who

---

[4] Jazmine Lawrence was an Air Combat Systems Officer on the Sea King helicopters on Canada's East Coast.
[5] See 1 Corinthians 15:21–26, 2 Timothy 1:9–10.

> He has saved us and called us to a holy life—not because of anything we have done but because of his own purpose and grace. This grace was given us in Christ Jesus before the beginning of time, but it has now been revealed through the appearing of our Savior, Christ Jesus, who has destroyed death and has brought life and immortality to light through the gospel.
> **2 TIMOTHY 1:9–10**

loved him, and were part of his father's flock. He said unless we became like children we could not enter his kingdom. He taught that his kingdom was near, though not of this world. It was currently and eternally good news and could be experienced on earth as well as in heaven. I've included an overview of categories and Scripture on the Kingdom of Heaven in Appendix B if you would like to study this more.[6]

In what we call The Lord's Prayer, we quote Jesus saying, "Your kingdom come, your will be done on earth as it is in heaven" (Matthew 6:10). We are asking that there be an infusion of what we were made for into what we are currently experiencing. We're praying for the perfect to intersect with our imperfection, for justice to overcome our injustice, and for peace to rule amidst our chaos. Yes, that eternal kingdom is real, but not yet fully here. We live in the perpetual advent of the "already but not yet." Living in this tension requires courage.

With my own eyes I have seen the blinding blue waters of the Adriatic Sea, the breath-taking grandeur of the Swiss Alps, and the glowing green of tropical trees in a friend's backyard in Thailand. This earth is beautiful. I've also wondered what those shapes, colors, and majesty will look like on the new earth. I am quite sure I'll need my new eyes in my glorified body in order to really see.[7]

Everything we observe and experience on this planet is under the curse. Even in its most beautiful state, it is not what it was nor what it will be. This could drive us to despair or propel us to hope. Because—we know how the story ends. History = His Story! We have details about the final battles.

---

6 See Appendix B.
7 See Romans 8:3–31, Philippians 3:20–21, 1 Peter 1:21.

We know Who will win the ultimate war. Talk about a vibrant and violent soundtrack—read the last book of the Bible—Revelation.

Revelation not only describes apocalyptic battles, judgments, beasts, bowls, and trumpets, it also gives us glimpses of our forever home. Here in the new heaven and the new earth, Eden is restored, the curse is lifted, the glory of every nation is honored, and the Messiah, King Jesus, reigns forever.[8]

PERSPECTIVE

What battles are you facing today? What enemies stay so close that it seems you must eat your lunch in the midst of them? You know, like "He prepares a table before me in the presence of my enemies."[9] What anxiousness is suffocating for you right now? "Why, my soul, are you downcast? Why so disturbed within me?"[10] What relationships are in turmoil?

Is it possible to lift your head and take a look at the bigger picture? What do you see when you look back all the way to Eden and God's Story coming toward you? What do you see when you look up right now into God the Father's loving face or when you grab onto the nail-scarred hand of your Savior, King Jesus? What do you see when you look forward beyond your earth-time and into eternity?

Let us face the spiritual warfare of this day, one day at a time, with kingdom courage.

> And for us this is the end of all the stories and we can most truly say that they all lived happily ever after. But for them it was only the beginning of the real story. All their life in this world and all their adventures in Narnia had only been the cover and the title page. Now at last they were beginning Chapter One of the Great Story, which no one on earth has read, which goes on forever, in which every chapter is better than the one before.[11]
> —C.S. Lewis, *The Last Battle*

---

8 See Revelation chapters 12 and 22.
9 See Psalm 23:5.
10 See Psalm 43:5.
11 Lewis and Baynes, *The Last Battle*, 173–174.

CHAPTER 11

Jesus Loves Me

A SONG FOR EVERYONE

ROWING ACROSS THE Hudson River to Constitution Island, West Point cadets were welcomed Sunday after Sunday with freshly made tea or lemonade, ginger cookies, and Bible study. At the home of sisters Susan and Anna Warner, these young men were taught deep spiritual and practical truth. Often, they would also learn a new hymn Anna had composed.[1]

One of these songs started as a poem Anna wrote in 1860 for a tender chapter about a dying child in her sister's novel, *Say and Seal*.[2] In 1862, the choirmaster and composer, William Batchelder Bradbury, learned of the poem and added a tune as well as a chorus.[3]

> Jesus loves me, this I know,   Yes, Jesus loves me.
> For the Bible tells me so.   Yes, Jesus loves me.
> Little ones to Him belong,   Yes, Jesus loves me,
> They are weak, but He is strong.   The Bible tells me so.

---

[1] Bethanne Kelly Patrick, 2017.
[2] Warner and Warner, *Say and Seal, Volume I*, 115–116.
[3] Ule, "Who Wrote "Jesus Loves Me?"

Translated into many languages, "Jesus Loves Me" has been one of the most familiar songs among Christians around the world for more than 150 years. Military cadets sang it in their rowboats and then later in foxholes. Mothers and fathers still sing it to their children. Theologian Karl Barth is said to have summed up all his writings about God and the Scripture with: "Jesus loves me, this I know, for the Bible tells me so."[4]

I am inspired by the story of these two unmarried sisters whose mother died when they were young, and whose father in financial hardship, moved them to their country home on Constitution Island near where their uncle had been the chaplain at West Point from 1828–1838. While both were prolific authors (Susan's book *The Wide, Wide World* was the second most popular novel of its time, after *Uncle Tom's Cabin*), their military ministry was a priority and a joy. For the last ten years of her life, Susan was the main Bible teacher on Sunday afternoons. Then Anna kept teaching for three more decades, the last year of her Sunday Bible class likely including a senior cadet who would become a General and a President, Dwight D. Eisenhower.[5] It is not a stretch to conclude that through all those years young soldiers learned the song and the truth, "Jesus Loves Me."

The Warner sisters chose to live very simply to maintain their home and the island as a place of ministry to cadets. They turned down multiple offers from those who wished to buy it to create an amusement park. This dedication resulted in a gift that is still giving today. A woman known as Mrs. Russell Sage bought the island from Anna some years after Anna's father and sister had passed. Then Mrs. Sage wrote to President Roosevelt in 1908, offering to deed the island to the government with the stipulation that it "be for the use forever of the United States Military Academy at West Point . . . and that Miss Anna Bartlett Warner have the right to reside as at present . . . thereto during her natural life."[6] Note the president's kind and dignified letter to Anna.[7]

---

4 "Karl Barth." Christianity Today, Christian History.
5 Patrick, 2017.
6 Egleston Phelps Stokes, *Letters and Memories of Susan and Anna Bartlett Warner*, 47–54.
7 Egleston Phelps Stokes.

MY DEAR MISS WARNER,
I have written to Mrs. Sage thanking her, and I write to you to thank you and her to make this gift to the Nation. You have rendered a real and patriotic service, and on behalf of all our people I desire to express our obligation and our appreciation. With regard, believe me,

>Sincerely yours,
>(Signed) THEODORE ROOSEVELT

What is it that makes the love of Jesus so essential to people of all ages around the world? And why is it especially important when we consider the march and music of military in the Bible? Knowing, believing, and living in the love of Jesus bolsters our courage—and so much more.

HIS LOVE SHAPES OUR IDENTITY

Love tells us who we are and to Whom we belong. Living as a loved one directs our behavior and guides our relationships with other loved ones. Do we know how very much we are loved? Is love the very music of our lives?

David and I have been friends since 1980 and married since 1986 (and still good friends!). Almost every day of our marriage we have said to each other, "I love you." Often, when David says to me, "I love you," I reply with, "Love you too!" But one day after that exchange as he walked by me in the kitchen, he stopped, gently lifted my chin, looked into my eyes and slowly said, "I. Really. Love. You." I didn't have the same quipped reply, "Love you too!" I wasn't sure what to say—it was wonderful and maybe a bit uncomfortable—but I believed him.

Whether or not a person has ever directly expressed this kind of love to you in words, please hear God say it as he looks into your eyes with kindness, "I. Really. Love. You." Then keep embracing those words from the God of the universe—because they are true.

> See what great love the Father has lavished on us, that we should be called children of God! And that is what we are!
> —1 John 3:1a

> Therefore, as God's chosen people, holy and dearly loved, clothe yourselves with compassion, kindness, humility, gentleness and patience. Bear with each other and forgive one another if any of you has a grievance against someone. Forgive as the Lord forgave you. And over all these virtues put on love, which binds them all together in perfect unity.
> —Colossians 3:12–14

HIS LOVE SAVES OUR HUMANITY

Jesus who is Love came after us, called us, and bought us with his own perfect human blood. We didn't have to earn his love or this redemption. In our broken and sinful state, he believed we were worth rescuing. And we were not just rescued to then be sent on our way—but to be drawn into a daily life-long love relationship with our Savior who has good purposes for each of us.

> You see, at just the right time, when we were still powerless, Christ died for the ungodly. Very rarely will anyone die for a righteous person, though for a good person someone might possibly dare to die. But God demonstrates his own love for us in this: While we were still sinners, Christ died for us.
> —Romans 5:6–8

> But because of his great love for us, God, who is rich in mercy, made us alive with Christ even when we were dead in transgressions—it is by grace you have been saved. And God raised us up with Christ and seated us with him in the heavenly realms in Christ Jesus, in order that in the coming ages he might show the incomparable riches of his grace, expressed in his kindness to us in Christ Jesus. For it is by grace you have been saved, through faith—and this is not from yourselves, it is the gift of God—not by works, so that no one can boast. For we are God's handiwork, created in Christ Jesus to do good works, which God prepared in advance for us to do.
> —Ephesians 2:4–10

HIS LOVE SECURES OUR ETERNITY

As the song *Beautiful Name* boldly proclaims, "You didn't want heaven without us, so Jesus you brought heaven down."[8] How is it that we are loved so much that God desires to spend forever with us? It's true! If it was not true, he would not have gone through the womb, the cross, the grave, and the empty tomb to pursue us. We are a treasure whom Jesus cherishes, more than we will ever understand, but must believe.

> For God so loved the world that he gave his one and only Son, that whoever believes in him shall not perish but have eternal life. For God did not send his Son into the world to condemn the world, but to save the world through him.
> —John 3:16–17

HIS LOVE CENTERS OUR THEOLOGY

The love of Jesus is both just and generous. It is steadfast and unfailing. And even though there are places in the Bible that are difficult and raw, as well as times in our lives that are unexplainable and unbearable, there is a perfect Love that holds it, and us, all together and will never be anything other than loving. This truth centers everything we believe.

> Whoever does not love does not know God, because God is love. This is how God showed his love among us: He sent his one and only Son into the world that we might live through him.
> —1 John 4:8-9

> For I am convinced that neither death nor life, neither angels nor demons, neither the present nor the future, nor any powers, neither height nor depth, nor anything else in all creation, will be able to separate us from the love of God that is in Christ Jesus our Lord.
> —Romans 8:38–39

---

[8] *What A Beautiful Name* - Hillsong Worship. https://www.youtube.com/watch?v=b6snOj0oZDU.

> And I pray that you, being rooted and established in love, may have power, together with all the Lord's holy people, to grasp how wide and long and high and deep is the love of Christ, and to know this love that surpasses knowledge—that you may be filled to the measure of all the fullness of God.
> —Ephesians 3:17b–19

HIS LOVE HELPS MAKE SENSE OF OUR SUFFERING

There is something about love that not only carries us through heartbreak but makes it possible for heartbreak to grow our capacity for joy.[9] Until we get to heaven, suffering will be part of our stories. Jesus did not sugar coat it when He said in John 16:33, "In this world you will have trouble. But take heart! I have overcome the world." This means that nothing gets past the love of Jesus, and nothing gets the final say in this world except for the love of Jesus.

Military members carry out their responsibilities while not expecting to be comfortable. Their mission includes hardship and necessitates resilience. It is fitting that the Apostle Paul connects discipleship—trusting reliable people with the reliable truths of Christ—with being a soldier of Christ.[10] As my mentor, the late Dr. Pam Reeve, often said, "God never wastes his servants' time nor their tears."

> Therefore, since we have been justified through faith, we have peace with God through our Lord Jesus Christ, through whom we have gained access by faith into this grace in which we now stand. And we boast in the hope of the glory of God. Not only so, but we also glory in our sufferings, because we know that suffering produces perseverance; perseverance, character; and character, hope. And hope does not put us to shame, because God's love has been poured out into our hearts through the Holy Spirit, who has been given to us.
> —Romans 5:1–5

---

9 Jerry Sittser, *A Grace Disguised*, 40–43.
10 2 Timothy 2:1–4.

HIS LOVE SHOWS US OUR POSSIBILITIES

Because we are loved, we are able to offer love. Because we are loved, we are bold. Because we are loved, we can move about this planet with a sense of security and significance that does not depend upon our relationships and accomplishments. We are free because we are loved.

> For Christ's love compels us, because we are convinced that one died for all, and therefore all died. And he died for all, that those who live should no longer live for themselves but for him who died for them and was raised again.
> —2 Corinthians 5:14–15

> This is how we know what love is: Jesus Christ laid down his life for us. And we ought to lay down our lives for our brothers and sisters. If anyone has material possessions and sees a brother or sister in need but has no pity on them, how can the love of God be in that person? Dear children, let us not love with words or speech but with actions and in truth.
> —1 John 3:16–18

> All glory to him who loves us and has freed us from our sins by shedding his blood for us. He has made us a Kingdom of priests for God his Father. All glory and power to him forever and ever! Amen.
> —Revelation 1:5b–6 (NLT)

A LOVE FOR EVERYONE

This great love of Jesus is for everyone—for every person, nation, military, civilian, good guy, bad guy, child, adult, saint, and sinner. This love has no boundaries and no deal-breakers. It must only be received. This love is a gift from a perfect God who

> For I am convinced that neither death nor life, neither angels nor demons, neither the present nor the future, nor any powers, neither height nor depth, nor anything else in all creation, will be able to separate us from the love of God that is in Christ Jesus our Lord.
> **ROMANS 8:38–39**

invites us all into relationship with him. This love takes care of the imperfectness of our beings and our stories, making it possible for us to be redeemed, reconciled, and made whole, no matter where we have come from. This love makes it so that our final destination can be heaven—forever.

A dying child, a traumatized soldier, a lonely sister, a frightened father, a sinful soul—anyone is welcomed at the cross of Jesus where the love of God was poured out for us. This solid truth frames not only our destinies, but also our earthly journeys. No matter what, we are loved. No matter the suffering, doubts, failures, or longings—Jesus loves us. And nothing can separate us from that love—no wars, no lies, no sin, no shame, no curse, no death.

Therefore, we march boldly into our callings, into our battles, and into our stories. We are courageous because we are completely, eternally, and irrevocably loved.

> Jesus loves me—loves me still,
> Though I'm very weak and ill.
> From his shining throne on high
> Comes to watch me where I lie.
>
> Jesus loves me—he will stay,
> Close beside me all the way.
> Then his little child will take,
> Up to heaven for his dear sake.
>
> Yes, Jesus loves me.
> Yes, Jesus loves me.
> Yes, Jesus loves me,
> The Bible tells me so.

Only two civilians are buried at the United States Military Academy at West Point: Susan Warner and Anna Warner. It was the cadets who requested this exceptional honor. The Warner home, "Good Crag," was willed to the academy and is now a museum.[11] Their song *Jesus Loves Me* lives on.

---

11 "North (Rear) Side - U. S. Military Academy, Warner House, Constitution Island, West Point, Orange County, NY."

CHAPTER 12

Until Then

WE HAVE TALKED about God's Story from Eden to heaven, about our created purposes, continual battles, and kingdom priorities. We have seen God's stunning movement in and through military in the Bible, listened to the music of God's grand theme of loving redemption, and considered his call on all Christ-followers to be spiritual warriors. As we now gather courage for the days to come, I want to focus on our mindset and marching orders.

Let's look first at this hymn written in 1958 by Stuart Hamblen.[1]

> My heart can sing when I pause to remember
> A heartache here is but a stepping stone
> Along a trail that's winding always upward,
> This troubled world is not my final home.
>
> But until then my heart will go on singing,
> Until then with joy I'll carry on,
> Until the day my eyes behold the city,
> Until the day God calls me home.

---

1 "Until Then," Hymnary.org.

Mr. Hamblen encouraged us to see that there is something very powerful about an "until then" mindset. It can help us get through whatever heartbreak, challenge, or monotonous situation in which we find ourselves.

MISSION READY

One of the disciplines of the military that I admire is their mission readiness. They are always working to stay sharp, improve their skills, maintain their equipment, and be ready to respond quickly and appropriately to any threat. They are not idle in between battles. They understand the importance of making good use of time when not on the front lines.

Remember our friend, TSgt Carnegie? While he has been deployed to military hot spots, most of his time has been spent making sure that measuring devices are accurate. He understands that his work is important in the grand scheme of things, whether it is ever seen or understood. He carries out his calling with excellence as an Airman and with joy as a committed follower of Christ.

We do not know when crisis or battle will come. We are not given a preview or an advanced memo in order to be prepared. How we live out each ordinary day is all the preparation we get for an emergency. What is already inside our minds and hearts—our spiritual reflexes—is what we have to work with when life as we know it is turned upside down. It is important for us to be intentional about our daily choices, our personal spiritual training, and long-haul faithfulness. TSgt Carnegie puts it like this, "The time to get ready is not when the attack comes; it's long before then. If you have not been consistent with your preparations, you will fail in the time of crisis."

THE LONG HAUL

Parenting comes to my mind as a good example of the long-haul faithfulness we are all called to, whether or not we are parents. Raising a child takes years, and parenting adult children is a whole other adventure. Even if those years seem to go by quickly, as the saying goes, the days can be quite long, especially when the children are very young.

David and I had the honor of raising four wonderful humans, each one unique and interesting, delightful and complex. As the parent who worked at home most of the time when the children were young, I remember many days when I felt like all I had to show for that day was the dirty diaper count. I knew then in my head what I now know deep in my heart—changing diapers is holy work. It is important. It is loving. It is necessary. The children are worth it. But at the time, contentment was a struggle for me some days. Am I glad that I was faithful—and hopefully cheerful—in that season? Absolutely!

MARCHING ORDERS FOR THE IN BETWEEN

Whatever the work God has called you to do, however long the days or mundane the tasks, mission readiness is just as important as mission accomplished. Here are seven encouragements I leave with you as you finish this book and carry on with your callings.

1. Walk Worthy

God's people are challenged in the Bible to walk worthy of God's ways, worthy of his call, worthy of the gospel, and worthy of the Lord. While we could carefully unpack each of these callings to worthiness, I will instead give you my summary.

In Deuteronomy 10:12–13 we are called to walk worthy of God's ways. In the context of the verses, it means our pattern of life is to be one of love and obedience to God. God will not play games with us. If he wants us to confess something or deal with an issue, he will tell us. But when he does, we need to respond. I think often God does not reveal more to us until we have followed what he has already communicated.

Walking worthy of his call in Ephesians 4:1 asks us to keep learning to get along and to never stop growing up. We cannot do this on a mountain top by ourselves. We need each other. We each have our part to contribute to working together well. I challenge us to be cautious about assuming we have arrived, and instead, keep maturing. While we can never determine nor control another person's behavior, we are always responsible for our own.

I have had the privilege of bearing witness to the lives of all eight of the founders of Cadence International. I can testify that each of them walked with Jesus in long-haul obedience. As I write this, two of the eight are still on this earth and in their 90s. Even as one struggles with dementia, her daughter recently told me that her mom is clearest when she prays.

Walking worthy of the gospel of Christ, as Paul urges us in Philippians 1:27, will include standing together and suffering. There is honor in suffering for what is right. Just ask a military person.

Then, we are asked to walk worthy of the Lord in Colossians 1:10–12. In this we live to please God and keep walking—keep persevering. We are walking this way because God has "qualified us to share in the inheritance of the saints in the kingdom of light." What an honor!

2. Work diligently

I think it is important to remember that work was given to humans before The Fall.[2] Work is something we are made for. While the struggle is real because of the curse, the satisfaction of a job well done is legitimate.

Furthermore, the Bible is clear that people have different talents, abilities, and giftings. Everyone is needed in God's kingdom work, and how each of us carries out our work affects others.[3] As Paul reminds us: "Work willingly at whatever you do, as though you were working for the Lord rather than for people" (Colossians 3:23 NLT).

3. Wage spiritual war fearlessly

Like it or not, we do not get the option of being spiritual pacifists. There are ongoing battles in the seen and unseen realms. We are part of them. If we are followers of Christ, we have spiritual responsibilities. We will be targeted and attacked by the enemy of our souls. Count on it. But do not be defeated by it. We are "more than conquerors" through Christ.[4]

One of the most repeated commands in the Bible is, "Fear not." The specific wording varies but the message is the same throughout the Old and New Testaments. In Isaiah 41:10 God is speaking: "So do not fear, for I am with you; do not be dismayed, for I am your God. I will strengthen you and help you; I will uphold you with my righteous right hand."

Connected to the command, we see that the presence of God—God with us, for us, in us—is the reason we do not need to let fear be in charge. God is in charge. Of course there are times we will feel afraid, as the warrior David

---

2 See Genesis 2:15.
3 See 1 Corinthians 12:12–31.
4 See Romans 8.

THE ADMIRAL'S CORNER

A Final Encouragement

For Followers of Jesus, there is a battle that we face each day. Romans 7:23 reminds us that daily there is a war being waged against our minds. In the military, cyber warfare has been growing significantly in importance and impact over the last 20 years. In a similar vein, that "spiritual hacker," Satan, is working routinely to hack and install malware to plant evil thoughts and temptations, to destroy the godly data that we have stored in our mind, and to "disrupt service" by attempting to distract our minds from keeping our focus on Jesus. This is a battle each of us needs to engage in *one day at a time*.

Romans 8:1 reminds us that even when we fall short in our efforts (which we will), "there is no condemnation" for those who trust in Christ. And Jesus has given us a "battle buddy" to guide and fight beside us each day—the Holy Spirit. As Joyce has reminded us, as we go through the day, we need to keep in mind that "nothing can ever separate us from God's love" (Romans 8:38–39). Absorb that please—*nothing*. Break it down further—*no thing* can *ever* break or lessen God's love for us.

And so, as we face our spiritual battles each day, may we rejoice in and cling to God's unconditional love for us. "Step up" with the Holy Spirit guiding you and defend well the territory of your mind and faith with the full armor of God. Just do that today; win the battle *this* day. Then come back tomorrow, again focused on "winning the battle today."

recounts, "*When* I am afraid." But we can also choose what David did, "I put my trust in You" (Psalm 56:3).

Jesus says in John 14:27, "Peace I leave with you; my peace I give you. I do not give to you as the world gives. Do not let your hearts be troubled and do not be afraid."

4. Welcome adversity

These verses from 2 Timothy 2:3–4 bear repeating here. "Join with me in suffering, like a good soldier of Christ Jesus. No one serving as a soldier gets entangled in civilian affairs, but rather tries to please his commanding officer."

Christians have a counter-intuitive take on hardship. It is not that we ask for trouble or celebrate suffering. We are not denying the harsh realities of life. However, throughout the stories of the Bible, we see our just and loving God turning all kinds of bad situations into ultimate good. We see him walking close to his people through their trials, not necessarily taking them out of the suffering, but making himself known to them in and through it. We observe that a deeper and richer life is a possible result of hearts and stories shaped by pain. We understand that resurrection is on the other side of death.

In a military sense, I also see that the devil in his scheming tends to target people who are dangerous to him and his ways. Even though his power is limited, he can certainly harass, discourage, and outright attack followers of Christ. Today as I write, we've had a car break down and towed, a family relationship in crisis, and significant work challenges. I am not suggesting the enemy caused any of these adversities; it does not matter their source. What matters is how we choose to respond—with panic or patience, anger or prayer, whining or wisdom. We have multiple chances to strengthen the muscle of faith when in adversity. "And without faith, it is impossible to please God" (Hebrews 11:6a).

5. Wonder reverently

I am grateful to live in a home with a beautiful view in a city where glorious sunsets over the mountains are common. Yet you might be surprised at how many times over the years one of my family members has called out to me (or texted) to say, "Look out the window now!" Sometimes those messages come with an added, "Stop what you're doing and look." While

God is freshly painting the sky, I can often be found with my head down, working on whatever it is that I find so important in the moment. I need help to lift my eyes and receive the beauty God is giving us and our whole city in the sunset.

Our grandchildren are helping me appreciate wonder in new ways. Seeing their faces light up—over a simple joy, a word spelled or understood, a loving eye contact—awakens my heart. Jesus said, "Truly I tell you, unless you change and become like little children, you will never enter the kingdom of heaven" (Matthew 18:3).

I remember when one of our granddaughters, Rilyn, was about five and decided she wanted to sit in the aisle seat at church so she could "close my eyes and lift my hands when I sing." (Apparently, we were somehow in her way when she was in the middle of the row.) Her young heart, already responsive to Jesus, knew the power and priority of worship.

Reverence for God centers our souls. We are never too old for wonder. And this posture invites a grateful spirit which helps us to more fully live with joy in the midst of brokenness.

6. Win lovingly

The stakes are high in military battles. Precious lives are in harm's way. Borders, power, safety, livelihoods, and futures are determined by the results of military engagements and negotiations.

Most of us will never have the future of a nation dependent upon us. But we who follow Christ have all been entrusted by him with a mission that affects eternity. It is this: "Go out and train everyone you meet, far and near, in this way of life, marking them by baptism in the threefold name: Father, Son, and Holy Spirit. Then instruct them in the practice of all I have commanded you. I'll be with you as you do this, day after day after day, right up to the end of the age" (Matthew 28:18–20 MSG).[5]

Jesus has won the battle for our redemption on the cross. But the battle for the souls of all people of the world rages on. Every one of us can have a part in winning them for Jesus as we open our arms wide and love those in our circles of influence in practical ways.

---

[5] Eugene Peterson, *The Message*, an English Bible paraphrase.

Which neighbor needs you to pray for them before they go into surgery? Which child needs an invitation to come have snacks at your house or dinner around your table? Which colleague needs to hear your affirmation of their excellent effort? What teammates need your prayer as they get deployed? Which friend of a friend needs your act of kindness today?

Through the years, after I prayed for them in the moment over an upcoming surgery or difficult situation, neighbors have said that they had never been prayed for like that before. I've heard some of our kids' friends say that they never had a family meal around a table until they shared dinner at our house. Through the years I've received more than one thank you message from friends who are now young adults for whom I bought shoes or clothes when they needed them as kids for a theater production or concert at school. Colleagues have expressed that my words or notes of encouragement meant more than I'll ever know.

These are not grand and glorious gestures, nor do they appear powerful in the battle for souls. But in God's kingdom economy, our loving actions day after day after day make an eternal difference. Let's not hold back.

7. Wait patiently

> Dear friends, don't ignore this fact: One day with the Lord is like a thousand years, and a thousand years are like one day. The Lord isn't slow to do what he promised, as some people think. Rather, he is patient for your sake. He doesn't want to destroy anyone but wants all people to have an opportunity to turn to him and change the way they think and act.
>
> The day of the Lord will come like a thief. On that day heaven will pass away with a roaring sound. Everything that makes up the universe will burn and be destroyed. The earth and everything that people have done on it will be exposed.
>
> All these things will be destroyed in this way. So think of the kind of holy and godly lives you must live as you look forward to the day of God and eagerly wait for it to come.
> —2 Peter 3:8–12a NOG

Time and timing are both gifts from God who sees from the beginning to the end of our earth-lives and all of history. These Bible verses point us again to the magnificent military victory God will accomplish when he determines the time is right. In the meantime, we are called to live in a way that honors him as we wait patiently, even as God himself is patiently waiting for us.

In chapter one I stated that God is the first and the last to use military force. In Eden, it was a cherubim with a flaming sword. For us and our salvation, it was Christ on the cross and then conquering the tomb. In heaven it will be Christ again—one warrior, one weapon, one encompassing victory. "I saw heaven standing open and there before me was a white horse, whose rider is called Faithful and True. With justice he judges and wages war . . . His name is the Word of God . . . Coming out of his mouth is a sharp sword . . ." (Revelation 19:11, 13b, 15a). Jesus will conquer the devil and his minions with his voice. He will do away with death and usher in the new heavens and the new earth—including a restored Eden with the tree of life. "On each side of the river stood the tree of life, bearing twelve crops of fruit, yielding its fruit every month. And the leaves of the tree are for the healing of the nations. No longer will there be any curse" (Revelation 22:2b–3a).

No longer will there be any curse! No longer will there be any enemies! No longer will there be any pain, shame, brokenness, and sin! The nations will be healed! This is how the earth-Story ends, even as it begins the rest and best of the eternal Story—a Story set to the music of Love that never stops.

In the meantime, we march to the cadence of God's heartbeat as royal representatives of him. We will not be exempt from battle or suffering. But it will all one day be made right by our good and loving God.

I started this chapter with lyrics from a hymn. I am ending this chapter, and this book, with my own attempt to capture in verse what it means for me to live with the perspective of "Until Then."[6]

---

6 "Until Then," ©Joyce Schroeder, 2021.

UNTIL THEN

Until then I watch and wait
In between Eden and Glory
My feet planted on this earth
Living well my one story

Life a mix of joy and pain
Never feel quite settled
Restless longing for the time
When there's no more battle

Until then I'll not give up
Knowing I have meaning
Purpose, plans, and work to do
Loved ones on me leaning

Christ himself has paved the way
Walked this earth path too
Took upon him the depths of sin
Gave me a heart that is new

Until then I stand in hope
Holy Spirit with me
No matter what the suffering is
Live in light of eternity

Then one day the best will start
No more war or pain
Courage and trust in Christ alone
From now until then

Acknowledgments

WHAT BEGAN AS a personal Bible study for a conference devotional I was giving over five years ago, beckoned me to look closer, think deeper, and understand more fully the significance of military in the Bible. What I discovered was fortifying, challenging, encouraging, and something I wanted to share with you. But I did not take this journey alone. Early drafts feedback from Dr. Jim Howard (theology), Jerri Kayll (framework), and Brian Kleager (military) were critical to the direction and momentum of this project. My husband David read the manuscript several times as it progressed, and he offered invaluable input and unwavering belief.

When Admiral Kemp began his editorial work, his comments evidenced extensive military knowledge and personal stories, and I reached out to ask if he would share his wisdom in his voice with us. I thank God for the gift of Curt's presence and encouragement to all who read this book. He is a testament to lived-out godliness expressed in a successful contemporary military career.

With each one who contributed edits—from punctuation to perspectives—the book you read is better, fuller, more accurate, and held for you with care by those mentioned above as well as Mike Paterson, Stacy Wiens, Kyrie Fuqua, Jazmine Lawrence, and Dr. Stan Fisher.

I've had the privilege of working with Kimberly Lamb on many projects for Cadence International. She is a gifted graphic designer and a lovely Christian with whom it is absolutely delightful to partner.

I want to acknowledge not only the allies who worked with me directly on this book during these years, but also some of those with whom I've had the honor of battling together for the Kingdom: Jessica, Alin, Joe, and Brent battling for righteous paths compelled by the love of Christ; Rebecca and our DenSem DMin professors and classmates for "charitable orthodoxy"; David's and my grown kids, their spouses, and our grandchildren battling for goodness wherever they live, learn, and work; Glory5! (Connie, Laura, Lori, and Jerri) battling in prayer; Cadence International staff sharing the gospel and our lives with military communities; and faithful ministry partners who for 40+ years have battled for us and our ministry outposts by their support, prayer, encouragement, and friendship.

Finally, from 1 Corinthians 15:57, "But thanks be to God! He gives us the victory through our Lord Jesus Christ."

APPENDIX A:

Thoughts on the Bible

THE BIBLE IS such a fascinating book—so complex and yet straightforward. So not politically correct or even age appropriate. So raw and honest, compelling and convicting.

I believe that the Bible is God's inspired Word, a beautiful result of God's Spirit breathing on and through humans, including their voices with his as he tells his Story to the world.

The Bible is not just a physical book; it is *alive*. How are we to ever comprehend, understand, and wrestle with this supernatural text?

ANCIENT AND CURRENT

The Bible was written over a 1500-year span by at least 40 different authors. The last book was written around 95 AD. This book is old!

Well preserved over all these years, scholars and archeologists have confirmed that the text we read today is, in fact, quite accurate to the earliest manuscripts we have of the text, which are in themselves ancient.[1]

The Bible was written from the perspective of the Ancient Near Eastern civilization in what is now the Middle East. Not one of its authors had a

---

[1] See *NLT Illustrated Study Bible*, p. 8–10, and *Holman Illustrated Bible Handbook*, p. 15–24, 301–311.

similar mindset or upbringing as my Western one. So how am I to approach this old and living sacred writing?

- With *humility*. Any know-it-all attitude, spiritual gift of discernment, well-studied education, or amazing life experience will never serve in the study of Scripture like humility. I want to sit tight in the conviction that no matter how much I know or understand, there is always more to know and understand. The Bible was inspired by God Almighty, nothing less. I am a human, nothing more.
- With *hunger*. Complacency is never my friend as I seek to know God and his Word. While I may continually build on the understanding I've gained through many years of reading and studying, my soul literally needs "Bible food" all the time—for the rest of my life.[2]
- With *help*. One of the Holy Spirit's jobs is to help us understand his Word. Since the day I put my faith in Christ as a young girl, his Holy Spirit has taken up residence inside of me—a wild and crazy true reality. I need to keep praying, keep listening, keep being corrected, and keep relying on God's Spirit for help. I also need help from wise and godly people who also study, write, speak, live, and wrestle with God's holy Word.

The Bible is also current. No, it is not still being written. It never will be Western. But it is so necessary and relevant to me and to my life today. In fact, it is relevant to any person any age from any country at any time in history. It. Is. Amazing.

There are places in the Bible I can drop into and feel like they are speaking directly to me for this very day. There are passages that I take comfort in, direction from, and stand on as foundations of my life that are timeless to me. And there are chapters I have read multiple times that I still do not fully understand or that do not make me feel comforted or strengthened. But those chapters are also from God. And I will keep reading and learning from them.

---

[2] Deuteronomy 30:14; All of Psalm 119, especially verse 103; Isaiah 59:21; Matthew 4:4; 1 Peter 2:1–3.

NARRATIVE AND DIRECTIVE

One of my favorite conversations is the one that happens when I give a friend his or her first Bible and explain how it works. We talk about how many authors wrote over a long period of time, how the Bible is not rated PG in many places, and how it is both human and divine. Then we go over the navigation system of this book—the table of contents, the two sides of the Book (Old Testament and New Testament), and the references (big numbers and little numbers).

I still smile thinking about one young friend's wide eyes when she heard about the names of the books within the book and the big and little numbers and exclaimed, "Oh, that's what a tattoo of John 3:16 means!"

Another important aspect to keep in mind is that this book is not necessarily chronological (nor are some books within the book chronological, like Jeremiah). So, we have a record of historical events from creation to the rebuilding of Jerusalem after the exile that go from Genesis to Nehemiah ending around 430 B.C.[3] Then the rest of the Old Testament books fall under the storyline of those historical books, kind of like puzzle pieces.

A similar phenomenon happens in the New Testament where we have historical events from Matthew through Luke with John fitting within the three synoptics, then Acts, followed by letters and a prophetic book.

Several literary genres are represented throughout the Bible, and these are also crucial to our understanding of what we are reading. We have history, poetry, and prophecy. We have eyewitness stories, researched historical accounts, and epistles (letters).[4]

Some books of the Bible, especially in the second half of the New Testament, are quite directive; not all rules per se, but lots of commands, examples, illustrations, and encouragements. They are also written to different ethnicities, so cultural context is important when studying. I highly recommend the IVP Bible Background Commentary, by Dr. Craig Keener.[5]

Think for a minute about how we sometimes get turned around if we expect all of the Bible to be directive, or if we don't understand the context of a narrative. Did we already say that the Bible is a complex book?

---

[3] *NLT Illustrated Study Bible*, A24, 859–862.
[4] I often reference the beautiful chart of how the books of the Bible fit with other events and civilizations in history in the *NLT Illustrated Study Bible*.
[5] Keener and InterVarsity Press, *The IVP Bible Background Commentary*.

SEEKING EARNESTLY, SEEING DIMLY

From the Old Testament book of Deuteronomy written around 1400 B.C.[6] to Jesus' words in the New Testament books of Matthew and Luke, God tells us that he can be known—that if we seek him, we will find him.[7] He is not a far-off deity who is playing hard to get. He is, in fact, pursuing us, and one of the ways he has done that is by giving us the Bible. There is great comfort and security in this. If we walk with God, we are not walking blindly through this pilgrimage called earthly life.

I think of it as a gold coin—a treasure of confidence. One side is confidence that we can truly know God, grow in wisdom, and walk in understanding as we seek God. The other side of this coin of confidence is that we will never know fully. In heaven so much will be clear, but we still will not know everything. I believe we will be studying this amazing book throughout eternity. As 1 Corinthians 13:12 says, "Now we see but a poor reflection as in a mirror; then we shall see face to face. Now I know in part; then I shall know fully, even as I am fully known."

In the meantime, I want to know more.

---

6 Note that two possible dates and subsequent chronologies exist for the exodus. See *NLT Illustrated Study Bible*, 134–136.
7 Deuteronomy 4:29, Matthew 7:7–8; Luke 11:9–10.

APPENDIX B:

The Kingdom of Heaven

THE KINGDOM OF HEAVEN IS LIKE A:
Farmer who sowed good seed in his field on four soils (Matthew 13:1–23)
Mustard seed (Matthew 13:31, Mark 4:30–32)
Yeast mixed into dough (Matthew 13:33)
Treasure hidden in a field (Matthew 13:44)
Merchant looking for fine pearls (Matthew 13:45)
Net let down to catch all kinds of fish (Matthew 13:47)
Owner of a house who brings out new and old treasures from his storeroom (Matthew 13:52)
King settling accounts with servants (Matthew 18:23–35)
Wedding banquet (Matthew 22:2–14)
Feast (Luke 13:29, 14:15)
Ten virgins with lamps going out to meet bridegroom (Matthew 25:1)
Farmer scattering seed and an enemy sowing weeds; both grow until harvest (Matthew 13:24–30 and 36–43, Mark 4:26–29)

THE KINGDOM OF HEAVEN IS GIVEN TO AND POSSESSED BY THOSE WHO ARE:
Poor in spirit (Matthew 5:3, Luke 6:20)
Persecuted for righteousness (Matthew 5:10)
Knowledgeable of the secrets of the kingdom of heaven given to you (Matthew 13:11, Luke 8:10)
Children (Matthew 19:14, Mark 10:14–15, Luke 18:16)
The Father's flock (Luke 12:32)
Those who love God (James 2:5)

THE ECONOMY OF THE KINGDOM OF HEAVEN:
Least in the kingdom are the ones who pick and choose from God's commands (Matthew 5:19)
Greatest in the kingdom are those who practice and teach all God's commands (Matthew 5:19)
Evil will be weeded out and the righteous will shine like the sun (Matthew 13:41–43)
Keys of the kingdom delegated to people (Matthew 16:19)
Must become like children to enter—position of child is greatest (Matthew 18:2–5)
Hard for the rich to enter (Matthew 19:16–26, Mark 10:23, Luke 18:24)
Tax collectors and prostitutes enter ahead of religious leaders (Matthew 21:31–32)
Pharisees shut the door of the kingdom of heaven in people's faces (Matthew 23:13)
Better to enter with one eye than have two eyes and be thrown into hell (Mark 9:47)
The one least in kingdom is greater than John the Baptist (Luke 7:28)
Might need to leave home and family for the kingdom (Luke 18:29–30)
Entered by being born again (John 3:3, 5)
God chose the poor in the eyes of the world to be rich in faith and to inherit the kingdom He promised to those who love Him (James 2:5)

DESCRIPTIONS OF THE KINGDOM OF HEAVEN:
It has come near (Matthew 3:2, 4:17, 10:7; Mark 1:15, Luke 10:9–11, 21:31)
Good news (Matthew 4:23, 9:35; Luke 4:43, 8:1; Acts 8:12)
On earth as it is in heaven (Matthew 6:10)
Feast (Matthew 8:10–11)
Has come upon you (Matthew 12:28, Luke 11:20)
Preached in the whole world as a testimony to all nations (Matthew 24:14, Luke 16:16)
Not something that can be observed (Luke 17:20)
Jesus will not drink from the fruit of the vine from the Last Supper until the Father's Kingdom has fully come (Matthew 26:29, Mark 14:25, Luke 22:18)
Coming with power (Mark 9:1)
Will never end (Luke 1:32–33)
In your midst (Luke 17:21)
Not of this world—from another place (John 18:36)
Not a matter of eating and drinking, but of righteousness, peace and joy in the Holy Spirit (Romans 14:17)
Not a matter of talk but of power (1 Corinthians 4:20)
Of Light (Colossians 1:12)
Of the Son God loves (Colossians 1:13)
Is appearing (2 Timothy 4:1)
Will be the scepter of justice of Jesus' kingdom (Hebrew 1:8)
Cannot be shaken (Hebrews 12:28)
Eternal (2 Peter 1:11)
The kingdom of the world has become the kingdom of our Lord and of his Messiah (Revelation 11:15)
Comes when the accuser is hurled down (Revelation 12:10)

PEOPLE AND THE KINGDOM OF HEAVEN:

Joseph of Arimathea waiting for the kingdom of God (Mark 15:43, Luke 23:50-51)
Jesus' followers are to proclaim his kingdom (Luke 9:1-2)
Not fit for the kingdom if one puts their hand to plow then looks back (Luke 9:62)
Seek his Kingdom and these things will be added to you (Matthew 6:33, Luke 12:31)
Conferred on his people by Christ (Luke 22:29-30)
Must go through many hardships to enter the kingdom of God (Acts 14:21-22)
Paul explaining about the kingdom of God (Acts 28:23)
Not to be inherited by wrongdoers (1 Corinthians 6:9-10, Galatians 5:19-21, Ephesians 5:5)
Flesh and blood cannot inherit the kingdom of God (1 Corinthians 15:50)
The Father has qualified us to share in the inheritance of his people in the kingdom of light (Colossians 1:12)
Co-workers for the kingdom (Colossians 4:10-15)
Called into his kingdom (1 Thessalonians 2:12)
Worthy of the kingdom and suffering for the kingdom (2 Thessalonians 1:5)
He made us to be a kingdom and priests to serve God (Revelation 1:6)
Suffering and kingdom and patient endurance go together (Revelation 1:9)
Believers will reign on the earth (Revelation 5:10)
His called, chosen, and faithful followers will be with the King of kings when he triumphs (Revelation 17:14)

JESUS IS THE KING:
King of the Jews (Matthew 2:2, 27:11, 27:29, 37, 42; Mark 15:2, 9, 12, 18, 26, 32; Luke 23:3, 37, 38; John 18:39, 19:3, 19)
Coming to you on a donkey (Matthew 21:5, John 12:15)
Blessed is the King who comes in the name of the Lord! (Luke 19:38)
King of Israel (John 1:49, 12:13)
Ruler of the kings of the earth (Revelation 1:5)
Will reign forever and ever (Revelation 11:15)
The Lamb is Lord of lords and King of kings (Revelation 17:14)
King of kings and Lord of Lords (Revelation 19:16)

GOD THE KING:
Eternal immortal, invisible, the only God (1 Timothy 1:17)
God the blessed and only Ruler, the King of kings and Lord of lords (1 Timothy 6:15)
King of the nations (Revelation 15:3)

MESSIAH, THE ANOINTED ONE:
Matthew 16:16
Mark 8:29
Luke 2:11
Luke 2:26
Luke 9:20
Luke 24:26, 46
John 4:25–26
John 11:24–27
John 20:31
Acts 2:36
Acts 5:42
Acts 18:28
Romans 9:5
Revelation 11:15
Revelation 12:10

Bibliography

Alcorn, Randy. *In Light of Eternity: Perspectives on Heaven.* Colorado Springs, Colorado: Eternal Perspectives Ministries, 1999.

Anderson, Ray S. *Minding God's Business.* Ray S. Anderson Collection. Eugene: Wipf and Stock Publishers, 2008.

Cadence International, Cadence.org.

Christian History | Learn the History of Christianity & the Church. "Karl Barth." https://www.christianitytoday.com/history/people/theologians/karl-barth.html.

Dickason, C. Fred. *Angels, Elect and Evil.* Chicago Illinois: Moody Bible Institute, 1975.

Dobson, Kent. *NIV First-Century Study Bible: Explore Scripture in Its Jewish and Early Christian Context.* London: Hodder & Stoughton, 2015.

Egleston Phelps Stokes, Olivia. *Letters and Memories of Susan and Anna Bartlett Warner.* G.P. Putnam's Sons, 1925.

Gunn, Robin Jones. *Sunsets.* Multnomah Publishers, Inc., 2000.

Holman Illustrated Bible Handbook. Holman Bible Publishers, 2012.

Imes, Carmen Joy. *Being God's Image: Why Creation Still Matters.* Downers Grove, IL: IVP Academic, 2023.

In Christ Alone (LIVE)—Keith & Kristyn Getty, 2020. https://www.youtube.com/watch?v=mshz89vfK3Q.

James, Carolyn Custis. *Lost Women of the Bible: The Women We Thought We Knew.* Grand Rapids, Michigan, Zondervan, 2005.

Keener, Craig S. and InterVarsity Press. *The IVP Bible Background Commentary: New Testament.* Second edition. Downers Grove, Illinois: InterVarsity Press, 2014.

Leston, Stephen. *Illustrated Guide to Bible Battles.* Ulrichsville, Ohio: Barbour Publishing, 2014.

Lewis, C. S. (Clive Staples), and Pauline Baynes. *The Last Battle*. 1st HarperTrophy ed. The Chronicles of Narnia, bk. 7. New York: HarperTrophy, 1994.

Library of Congress, Washington, D.C. 20540 USA. "North (Rear) Side—U. S. Military Academy, Warner House, Constitution Island, West Point, Orange County, NY."

Longman, Tremper. *How to Read Exodus*. Downers Grove, Ill.: IVP Academic, 2009.

Mowczko, Marg. "What's in a Name? Deborah, Woman of Lappidoth." *Marg Mowczko* (blog), November 27, 2015. https://margmowczko.com/deborah-woman-of-lappidoth/.

NLT Illustrated Study Bible. Carol Stream, Illinois: Tyndale House Publishers, Inc., 2015.

"Onward, Christian Soldiers." Wikipedia.org.

"Onward, Christian Soldiers." Hymnary.Org. https://hymnary.org/text/onward_christian_soldiers_marching_as.

Patrick, Bethanne Kelly. "What These Sisters Did to Become the Only Civilian Women Buried at West Point." Military.com, August 31, 2017. https://www.military.com/history/susan-and-anna-warner.html.

Patty, Tyler. "Curse and the Power of Blessing: A Linguistic Study of Genesis 1–11." Trinity Evangelical Divinity School, 2016.

Peterson, Eugene H.. *The Message: The New Testament in Contemporary English*. Colorado Springs, Colo.: NavPress, 1993.

Phil Wickham—Battle Belongs (Official Music Video), 2020. https://www.youtube.com/watch?v=qtvQNzPHn-w.

Press, Lexham. "Can We Know What Year Jesus Was Born?" Word by Word, December 16, 2021. https://www.logos.com/grow/what-year-jesus-was-born/.

Roos, Dave. "The Horrifying Discovery of Dachau Concentration Camp—And Its Liberation by US Troops." https://www.history.com/news/dachau-concentration-camp-liberation.

Schroeder, David. "The Word on the Word," 2016.

Schroeder, Joyce. "Joshua and the Tent." *JoyceSchroeder.com*, May 24, 2017.

Sittser, Jerry. *A Grace Disguised*. Grand Rapids, Michigan: Zondervan, 1995.

Spangler, Ann, ed. *The Names of God Bible*. Grand Rapids, Michigan: Revell, 2011.

Taps Bugler: Jari Villanueva. "WELCOME TO TAPS BUGLER." January 31, 2024. https://www.tapsbugler.com/.

That the World May Know. "Fertility Cults of Canaan." That the World May Know. https://www.thattheworldmayknow.com/fertility-cults-of-canaan.

Thompson, Curt. *The Soul of Shame: Retelling the Stories We Believe about Ourselves*. Downer's Grove, Illinois: IVP Books, an imprint of InterVarsity Press, 2015.

Ule, Michelle. "Who Wrote 'Jesus Loves Me?'" Michelle Ule, Author, May 28, 2019. https://www.michelleule.com/2019/05/28/jesus-loves-me/.

"United States Navy > About > Our Core Values." https://www.navy.mil/About/Our-Core-Values/.

"Until Then." Hymnary.org. https://hymnary.org/text/my_heart_can_sing_when_i_pause_to_rememb.

U.S. Department of Defense. "Despite COVID-19 Restrictions, Service Members Play Important Role in Inauguration."

Walton, John H. *The NIV Application Commentary: Genesis*. Zondervan, 2001.

Warner, Anna Bartlett, and Susan Warner. *Say and Seal, Volume I*, 2009. https://www.gutenberg.org/ebooks/28544.

Webb, William J., and Gordon K. Oeste. *Bloody, Brutal, and Barbaric?: Wrestling with Troubling War Texts*. Downers Grove, Illinois: IVP Academic, 2019.

What A Beautiful Name—Hillsong Worship, 2016. https://www.youtube.com/watch?v=nQWFzMvCfLE.

About the Authors

JOYCE SCHROEDER grew up as a missionary kid living in the Philippines, California, Colorado, and Germany. Her parents, Dick and Margaret Patty, are some of the founders of OCSC, now Cadence International (Cadence.org). She was part of the pioneering of Malachi Ministries in 1981, now Cadence Student Ministries. In 1995 her husband David became the president of Cadence and they have served from the Headquarters in Colorado since that time.

Joyce and David have four grown children, Kerith, Justin, Kyrie, and Jonathan, two sons-in-law (both named Jacob!), and six wonderful grandchildren so far. Who knew how much *joy* grandchildren would bring?!

Joyce has served in various ministry roles—teaching adult Bible classes, preaching, retreat speaking, directing Women's Ministries at church, as a Christian University board member, on the Communications Team of Cadence, and leading and participating in various initiatives, trainings, and writings. She worked part time as a substitute teacher in the local public schools, especially as the Schroeder kids were growing up. It was a great way to be in their world, get to know their friends, and be a loving light for Jesus.

She is a graduate of Multnomah University with a major in Biblical Studies, spent a year at Biola University for a K-12 teaching credential, and earned an MA in Biblical Counseling from Grace Seminary. Joyce has completed her coursework for a Doctor of Ministry in Leadership from Denver Seminary and is currently in the thesis phase. A DMin effort is what can happen when one asks the question, "What does my 80-year-old-self need from my 60-year-old-self?"

REAR ADMIRAL CURT KEMP is a 1972 graduate of the U.S. Naval Academy. After graduation, he served for 34 years in the Navy as a Surface Warfare Officer. He participated in the Vietnam War and in the first Gulf War, Desert Storm. During Desert Storm, he commanded a Navy destroyer that launched more Tomahawk missile strikes than any other ship. During his Navy career, he had the privilege to command five Navy organizations ranging in size up to 8,000 people, including command of a Carrier Strike Group.

After retiring from the Navy as a Rear Admiral, Curt moved to Leesburg, Virginia and for the next four years served as Chief Operating Officer of Prison Fellowship Ministries. From 2012 to 2022, he served as the Managing Chair in Northern Virginia for The C12 Group, America's leading resource for equipping Christian business owners and CEOs to *Build Great Businesses for a Greater Purpose*. He remains an advisor with C12 as Chair Emeritus.

Curt has been married to Ann Parsons Kemp since 1974. They have two adult children, Ian and Casey, and are blessed with five grandchildren. Curt and Ann are active members of Cornerstone Chapel in Leesburg, Virginia, where they participate in various ministries. Curt is a former Chairman of the Board of Directors at Cadence International.